Serena Williams: The Inspiring Story of One of Tennis' Greatest Legends

An Unauthorized Biography

By: Clayton Geoffreys

Visit my website at www.claytongeoffreys.com
Cover photo by Edwin Martinez is licensed under CC BY 2.0 / modified from original

Table of Contents

Foreword

Without a doubt, Serena Williams is one of the greatest women's tennis players of all time. Williams holds the record for the most Grand Slam titles in singles, doubles, and mixed doubles among all active players, with 39 Grand Slam titles at the time of this writing. In singles tournaments alone, Williams has 23 Grand Slam titles, making her the record-holder for the most by any tennis player in the Open Era. What makes Williams great is not only her sheer power and dominance on the tennis court, but her incredible degree of class and sportsmanship in both victory and in defeat. She is one of the most popular tennis players and with good reason: she's a great person on and off the court. What characterizes Serena Williams is her fiery ability to will her way out of tough situations in matches, while simultaneously remaining calm and strategic. Thank you for purchasing *Serena Williams: The Inspiring Story of One of Tennis' Greatest Legends*. In this unauthorized biography, we will learn Serena Williams' incredible life story and impact on the game of tennis. Hope you enjoy and if you do, please do not forget to leave a review!

Also, check out my website at claytongeoffreys.com to join my exclusive list where I let you know about my latest books. To thank you for your purchase, you can go to my site to download a free copy of *33 Life Lessons: Success Principles, Career Advice & Habits of Successful People*. In the book, you'll learn from some of the greatest thought leaders of different industries on what it takes to become successful and how to live a great life.

Cheers,

Clayton Geoffreys

Visit me at www.claytongeoffreys.com

Chapter 1: Serena Williams

She is the standard-bearer of women's tennis as we know it right now, and any argument about the greatest player in the sport, either man or woman, must include her. Seemingly everything about her is a lightning rod for controversy, from her on-court outfits to her pointed post-match interviews after losses and whether her powerful serve and forehand are even good for women's tennis.

Serena Williams is all of these things to all of these people. She has been the face of women's tennis for more than two decades, having enjoyed an unprecedented amount of success that has come with an equally unprecedented amount of scrutiny by both supporters and detractors alike. Few have been able to reach her level professionally, and fewer still can understand the weight she has carried as an African-American at the pinnacle of a sport so long dominated by white people.

She had a unique upbringing alongside older sister and fellow star Venus Williams while under the watchful eye of her outspoken and controversial father, Richard Williams, as well as her mother, Oracene Price. Serena Williams has brought many things to the WTA Tour, far more good than bad, and she has not lacked for attention at any point in her standout career. The sport has made her a worldwide star; her race has made her an ambassador for African-Americans and her philanthropy while doing both has made her a role model who is constantly in demand.

The holder of an Open Era-record 23 Grand Slam titles and 72 overall WTA Tour titles, current fiancée and expecting mother, Serena Jemeka Williams has lived quite the extraordinary life in just under 35 years.

Chapter 2: Early Life and Childhood

Serena Jemeka Williams was born September 26, 1981, in Saginaw, Michigan. She was the youngest of five children, having three half-sisters Yetunde, Lyndrea, and Isha Price, and full sister Venus Williams. Her father, Richard Williams, ran a private security firm, while her mother, Oracene Price, was a nurse.[1]

The idea to have tennis prodigies had come before both Venus and Serena were born. Richard Williams enjoyed watching tennis, and he noted that 1978 French Open women's champion Virginia Ruzici took home a top prize of $40,000, a substantial sum of money in that day and more than he made in a calendar year.[2]

Inspired to find a better life for his family, Williams dove into the instructional aspects of learning tennis despite having no background in the sport nor any coaching experience. He first taught his wife to play so that they could both hit balls with all five of their daughters.[3]

Despite being born in Michigan, the family would relocate to Compton, California, when the sisters were little. Compton is a suburb of Los Angeles infamously known as a high-crime area due to drugs and gang wars. Gunfire was a common occurrence in both the Compton area and around the hardscrabble tennis courts where the Williams sisters first learned how to hit tennis balls with their father.[4] Both sisters took an instant liking to the sport, though Serena claims in her autobiography that she hit balls with her mother more because

Venus liked the attention she got from her father when she practiced with him.[5]

The sisters had different body frames, with Venus long and lithe and Serena not so much, but both children were athletic. The elder sister could run a sub-5:30 mile by the age of eight, and both sisters were entered in tennis tournaments at the staggeringly young ages of 5 and 4, respectively.[6] The two would also watch hours of tennis videos with their father to learn strategy, namely how to exploit an opponent's weaknesses, and also proper footwork.[7]

The sisters quickly made a name for themselves on the USTA junior circuit in California, which did not break the siblings up into any age category and instead lumped them into the 12-and-under group. Richard Williams claims that Serena lost only three of the 49 tournaments she participated in between the ages of four and nine and made like Venus in being the number 1 player in that highly competitive circuit.[8]

But it was Venus' early success that started the path for the sisters to greatness. Her victory at the 10-and-under junior sectional championships in California in 1990 was her 17th title of the year, and she had dropped only nine games in five matches while doing so. The title also got her "promoted" to the 14-and-under division and club pros started to take notice of the skinny 5-foot-9 girl with the celestial name.[9]

"In the first place, she played like she was 16 years old," said Dorothy Cheney, one of the most famous players to come out of the California circuit. "She looked like she was 14. ....But boy oh boy, her game had everything. She was fast, she had a spin serve, she ran to the net, she had forceful groundstrokes, her anticipation was good, and her concentration was excellent. Boy, did she wax me!"[10]

Though Richard Williams was outspoken regarding his daughters' talent on the course like any doting father would be, it should be remembered he was always a father first. As the two sisters played their way up the ladder in California, part of the growing reputation meant that equipment and apparel representatives were also interested in these two African-American youngsters with seemingly limitless potential.

The world was still a year away from Gatorade's famous "Be Like Mike" ad that featured Michael Jordan, but his status as Nike's pre-eminent pitchman had long been established and was a beacon that all athletes could point to for inspiration.

This led Williams to phone Rick Macci, who at that point, was already a name in tennis circles in Florida for coaching Jennifer Capriati in her pre-teen years before she entered the WTA Tour at the age of 13 and found instant success.[11] Macci, though, had never heard of the Williams sisters and only found out about them because one of his friends had noted Richard Williams wanted to move the family to the Florida area to continue the girls' tennis training. A short while later, Williams called Macci, who described that phone call as "probably one of the most bizarre and interesting conversations I ever had in my life."[12]

Macci flew out to Compton for a weekend with the Williamses, one that set the groundwork for their eventual move to Florida. Their future coach saw the diamond-in-the-rough potential of both Venus and Serena. Richard Williams may have been a good teacher, but he was not a good tennis coach. As Macci noted, "technically, they were a train wreck."[13]

But the one area Macci noticed Williams helped highly develop and hone was the sisters' competitive nature. "The way they competed, and they didn't want to lose the point, to me their stock rose even more. To me, that's always the X factor, the way someone competes. Venus and Serena had a deep down burning desire to fight and compete at this age. It was unique. Unreal hunger."[14]

After some negotiations in which Williams was able to secure both an apparel deal and the use of a motor home in exchange for scholarships and a percentage of his daughter's future prize winnings, it was time for the Williams family to move to Florida.[15] The move went counter to the usual practices of the day in which kids would climb through the ranks of the USTA ladder and eventually be pro-ready by the age of 15 or 16, though Capriati was the exception to the rule Richard Williams hoped Venus could emulate.[16]

All this time, Serena was little more than an afterthought, but was also a very willing player who was eager to learn. And there would be plenty of time for learning with Macci, who put the sisters through a grueling training regimen of six hours of practice for six days a week over the next three-plus years.[17]

Macci realized that Serena would take longer to mature, but he was also willing to show that needed patience because, as he put it, she was "wired for greatness."[18]

"The one thing about Serena that always stood out to me was that she was fearless," Macci said. "She wasn't afraid to miss. And she *hated* to lose. She had to be first in everything, even if it was getting a drink of water. ... When she played tag, she played with a closed fist.

"That's how competitive this girl was. I told Richard one of two things was going to happen: She will be number 1 in the world, or she will go to jail. One (of those) two things can happen. And I'm serious ... but when you can get a girl to be that competitive, that athletic, and then you can lock in some good strokes – I knew no doubt that she (would) be number 1 in the world."[19]

What turned out to be the greatest weapon of Serena's career, her serve, needed little tweaking according to Macci. He noted she "had a natural throwing motion" and that he had known by age 10 that "Serena would have the best serve in the world."[20]

Not competing on the junior tour was a point of contention between Williams and Macci, but it was also the only time they had differing opinions on the girls' futures. Williams felt it was important not to have the daughters subjected to competitive pressure against each other, and no one had any idea how the public would respond to a pair of African-American teenagers potentially storming through the junior circuit to become tennis' next big thing.[21]

The decision, and how it turned out, is something Macci still marvels about to this day.

"Serena never played in any tournaments. No nationals. No local tournaments. Never got on a plane and played an ITF and left the country. ... Going out of the box or creating a whole new box, the path that they took was so unconventional. No tournaments. And people might say 'They were different' or 'They were athletes' or whatever, but they are the only ones that ever tried that."[22]

Unconventional. Unprecedented. Outside the box. Few realized how prescient these terms would be as a young teenager would take her first uncertain steps in a professional setting before going on to be one of the sport's greatest players.

Chapter 3: Early Professional Career

It should first be established that nothing about the beginning of Serena's career, or her sister's for that matter, qualifies as conventional. Because of the flameout of Jennifer Capriati, a one-time WTA Tour prodigy and 13-year-old pro in 1990 who burned out after four years and needed nearly five years after that to rediscover her game, the WTA instituted an age limit of 15 for the 1995 season.[23]

Serena's older sister Venus had been one of the last 14-year-olds on the WTA Tour the year prior, and the younger Williams had filed a lawsuit against the WTA Tour to allow her to play in the same tournament as Venus in Oakland in late October of 1995. Serena dropped that lawsuit at the request of her parents, but they had figured out a workaround to the age ban. A tournament in Quebec City, Canada, gave the younger Williams a wild-card entry to the qualifying round of its Tier III tournament.

Everything that Venus' debut was the year before – near the family home in Oakland and against a high-quality opponent in Grand Slam winner Arantxa Sanchez Vicario – Serena's first match as a professional was not. Even getting north the border proved problematic, mainly due to both Williams and her father missing their flight from Philadelphia because they lost track of time looking for souvenirs.[24]

As a result, they wound up in four different airports before arriving in Quebec late Friday night for her Saturday match. Many of Williams' rackets got lost in the luggage shuffle, and there was no time for her to practice before facing 18-year-old Anne Miller.

Miller, whose brief career ended at the age of 21 with a high-water mark of a third-round appearance in the 1998 U.S. Open, never won a WTA Tour title.[25] But in facing a naive ingénue such as Williams who had little grounding at any professional level of tennis, Miller may as well have been Chris Evert or Martina Navratilova.

Miller throttled Williams by a 6-1, 6-1 count in a mostly anonymous setting – the match was played as another match was contested simultaneously on the next court. The younger Williams held serve just once in the match and broke Miller just once. There were flashes of the raw power that had enthralled everyone and made people take notice of Serena Williams, but she also was a diamond in the rough that needed polish, and more importantly, match experience.

"She has as much power as anybody around, but maybe she needs to play some junior events the way Anna Kournikova has to learn how to become match-tough," Miller told the New York Times after the match. "There really is no substitute for the real thing. I felt like a complete veteran compared to her."[26]

For all of the controversy Richard Williams generated while he was raising his daughters to be tennis players who reached the pinnacle of their sport, the passage of time had also shown him to be rather prescient when it comes to how he dealt with his daughters growing up. He understood early that they were going to be headstrong, like him in some ways, but his quotes about Serena's play style and raising two teenage daughters playing tennis are interesting to revisit more than 20 years later:

"I'm just afraid, especially with Serena, who's a perfectionist, that she'll take it so seriously that she'll never have fun with it; be a flop at 18," he said in that New York Times article. "You can't really say no to these kids these days, not the way parents did in my day ... and to be honest, if I did, I'm afraid I'd lose them."[27]

Williams did not play a WTA Tour event in 1996, and there were still plenty of inconsistencies in her game as she played a limited schedule in 1997. She failed to advance through qualifying at three tournaments – first losing in straight sets to Alexia Dechaume-Balleret in the first round of the State Farm Evert Cup, then to Magui Serna in the quarterfinals of the Acura Classic and Dominique Monami in the second round of the European Indoor Championships.[28]

By this time, Williams was ranked 448th in the world and entered as a qualifier for the Kremlin Cup in Moscow. This time, she progressed through three rounds of qualifying – avenging a loss to Serna in the process – and entered the main draw. But in round 32, Williams fell to Kimberly Po, who was ranked 22nd in the world, 6-3, 7-6.[29] Her sister Venus would reach the quarterfinals, where she lost to top seed and eventual tournament champion, Jana Novotna.

The following week, Williams returned stateside and accepted a wild-card entry into the main draw of the Ameritech Cup in Chicago. In the first round, she defeated Russian Elena Likhovtseva in straight sets to earn a spot opposite fifth-seeded Mary Pierce. And the coming out party for the younger Williams sister began as she pulled off a 6-3, 7-6 upset to advance to the quarterfinals.[30]

There waited a bigger name in second-seeded Monica Seles, who had reached the semifinals of both the French Open and the quarterfinals of the U.S. Open that year.[31] After dropping the first set, Williams found her power game in her serve and stayed patient on the baseline to outduel Seles, breaking her three times in the decisive set of her 4-6, 6-1, 6-1 victory. Williams capped off the win in style by racing to a drop shot and sending it down the line before doing a dance to celebrate match point.

"I think a lot of balls she hit, a lot of players wouldn't get to," Williams said. "It feels kind of good. It's just a win. When I was little, I always wanted to play Monica."[32]

Third seed Lindsay Davenport would be Williams' semifinal opponent, and at 6-foot-2, Davenport was one of the more imposing players on the WTA circuit. She had also enjoyed a breakout season, making her deepest foray into a Grand Slam event by reaching the semifinals of the U.S. Open that year.[33] Davenport grabbed the first set by breaking Williams at 3-all, and Williams needed to take a medical timeout down 1-2 in the second set after spraining her ankle.

Still, Williams showed some resiliency after the injury and fought off a match point at 2-5 to break Davenport. She had a chance to level the set at 5-all but missed a backhand with all the court to use after catching Davenport out of position with a drop shot at 30-all.[34]

The 6-4, 6-4 defeat did plenty of good for Williams, though. She was the lowest-ranked player in the Open Era to defeat a pair of top 10 players in the same tournament. And by year's end, she would crack the top 100 in the WTA Tour rankings at No. 99.

"I bet it shocked a lot of people with how well they've done so soon, especially Serena," noted Davenport. "We've been hearing for so long about how great (Serena) is going to be, and then it's nice to finally see her play and to prove everybody right."[35]

Armed with her top 100 ranking, 1998 would mark the first year Serena Williams was a full-time player on the WTA Tour. She still had to take a qualifier's route to enter some tournaments, though, and that was the case in her first event of the year. At the Adidas International in Sydney, she rolled through three qualifying matches without dropping a set[36] before entering the main draw.

Here she proved her performance in Chicago was not a fluke as she upended seventh-seeded Sandrine Testud before avenging her loss to Davenport by rallying for a three-set victory. That ride would end with a semifinal loss to Sanchez Vicario, but it would be a big confidence boost ahead of the first major of the year, the Australian Open.

Williams was given a difficult draw, squaring off against sixth-seeded Romanian Irina Spirlea in the first round. Playing on center court in the same group draw as her elder sister, Serena outlasted a game and ousted Spirlea in three sets to win her first Grand Slam match. While also unseeded, Venus Williams coasted by Alexia Dechaume-Balleret to set up the first professional match between the siblings.[37]

The only other time Serena and Venus faced each other growing up was in 1990 when then 8-year-old Serena played her first junior tournament and reached the final. There, Venus recorded a straight-set victory.[38] This time, however, it would be a continent away from their California days with their mother Oracene watching from the crowd and maintaining a neutral stance as her daughters played on tennis' biggest stage.

The match played out as you would expect the personalities of the sisters would dictate. Serena tried to force the action as the more physical player of the two, but her eagerness would come back to haunt her. She had seven double-faults in the first set alone and squandered a set point. Still, the younger sister had the chance to win the tiebreak until a missed backhand gave Venus a 5-4 edge.

The older sister then dominated the early part of the second set, grabbing a 3-0 lead on her way to a straight-set win. Venus made like the good older sister, putting a consoling arm around Serena after they shook hands at the net and knowing full well that this was going to happen many, many times over, even if it was Serena offering the consoling.[39]

"If I had to lose in the second round, no better than to Venus," Serena said. "I tried to keep thinking of her as someone else, but I guess Venus has a little more experience than me."[40]

Venus Williams would get as far as the quarterfinals before losing to Davenport in three sets. For Serena, it continued her rapid rise in the WTA rankings. She had gone from No. 96 in Sydney to No. 53 in Melbourne to now No. 42 post-Australian Open.[41]

Between the first and second-round matches, the sisters felt like they were ready to take on anyone in tennis, with an emphasis on "anyone." The headstrong siblings went to the ATP offices in Melbourne and confidently announced to the officers that they could beat any man who was ranked in the vicinity of 200th on the men's side.

At the office that day was a German player named Karsten Braasch. He had gotten inside the top 40 on the ATP Tour, reaching No. 38 in 1994, but had since tumbled down the rankings to 203rd. Braasch was known for a fitness regimen that sorely lacked the fitness part – he would smoke cigarettes during changeovers and occasionally have a beer as well.[42]

Somewhat entertained by the sisters' brashness, Braasch accepted the challenge on the spot. The three worked out the arrangements for the match to be played at Melbourne Park, and it was agreed upon that he would face each sister for one set. Word quickly spread, and as a result, officials at the club were turning people away.[43]

Both matches were incredibly one-sided in Braasch's favor. He "warmed up" for the match by playing a round of golf and continued his trademark changeovers of cigarettes and beer. He took the first five games off Serena Williams and beat her 6-1 before dusting off Venus Williams 6-2.[44]

While Serena Williams was establishing herself as a Top-40 player capable of beating anyone on a given day, the breakthrough in which she had that consistency for an entire tournament was still lacking. She reached the quarterfinals in both Miami and Rome on different surfaces, first losing to world No. 1 Martina Hingis in three sets on the hard surfaces in Miami before suffering another straight-set loss to her sister on the clay in Rome.[45]

Her next major would be her first appearance at Roland Garros for the French Open. Now ranked 27th in the world, Williams again showed her brilliance as she routed 15th seed Dominique Van Roost 6-1, 6-1 to set up a fourth-round showdown with Sanchez-Vicario. It was an incredibly contentious match with the American teenager firing away at the veteran Spaniard.

Williams took the first set 6-4, drawing frustration from Sanchez Vicario as she slammed her racket. The Spaniard took a three-minute break in the second set trailing 2-3 to change outfits, something

Williams felt swung the momentum of the match. But the real truth is that Williams had two chances to close out the match first at 5-2 and 30-all on Sanchez Vicario's serve only to drop the next two points and again on her serve just three points from victory before the Spaniard rallied.

The match swung Sanchez Vicario's way as she won the second set and was up 4-2 when Williams laced a shot that fizzed by her ear and landed wide. The Spaniard claimed that Williams purposely tried to hit her and was put off afterward by what she felt was a lack of respect from the young upstart.[46]

"I just think she doesn't have respect," said Sanchez Vicario after she denied Williams a quarterfinal match opposite her sister Venus. "She cannot go in with that attitude. You know, I'm glad that I beat her. That's the thing – I taught her a lesson."[47]

The struggles against Sanchez Vicario would continue into the grass season as she dropped a three-setter in the quarterfinals in Eastbourne. Her first experience at Wimbledon came to an unexpected end in the third round when a calf injury forced her to retire in the second set against Virginia Ruano Pascual.[48] Though it prevented another potential Venus-Serena showdown in a Grand Slam event, the younger Williams was pleased with her first go-around at the all-England club.

"I had all the expectations for this Wimbledon," she said. "I expected to go all the way. I guess I just won't be able to this year. ... In the future, I definitely see myself as one of the champions."[49]

She probably did not mean the immediate future in singles because Williams picked up her first Grand Slam title in mixed doubles as she teamed up with Max Mirnyi to defeat Mahesh Bhupathi and Mirjana Lucic.[50]

Williams would get no further than the quarterfinals of her remaining three events that year and was eliminated in round 32 at the U.S Open in a three-set match against the ninth-seeded Spirlea, who avenged her defeat to Williams in Melbourne. Much like Wimbledon, Williams had her destiny in her hands, but a mishit backhand at 15-40 and 5-all in the third set spelled the end to her chances of advancing.[51]

By the end of her season, which concluded with a quarterfinal loss to Sandrine Testud in Filderstadt, Germany, Williams was ranked 19th on the WTA Tour. Bigger things were set to come the following year.

However, Australia was not where the progress was to be made. Williams lost to Steffi Graf in the second round in Sydney and round 32 to Testud at the Australian Open, dropping the third set 9-7. Williams thought she had won the match 8-6 when she hit a backhand down the line, but Testud pointed to a spot on the court where the ball appeared out, and umpire Laura Ceccarelli overruled the linesman.

Williams melted down after that, double faulted to fall behind 8-7, and after missing a backhand on match point, fired her racket at the net in disgust, prompting boos from the crowd in Melbourne. She denied that the overturned call contributed to the loss, blaming it more on the fact that she "didn't attack like I should have. If I lost a match over a bad call, that would be out of control."[52]

The fire from that loss would build for nearly a month before Williams' next tournament, the Open Gaz de France in Paris. She did not drop a match en route to the final, dispatching three Frenchwomen, including No. 2 seed Nathalie Tauziat and No. 7 seed Julie Halard-Decugis in the second round and quarterfinals. After beating Nathalie Dechy in the semis, there was one last French player separating Williams from her first WTA Tour title: sixth-seeded Amelie Mauresmo.[53]

The two had split the first two sets before Williams pushed ahead 4-1 in the third. Mauresmo, though, recovered and eventually forced a tiebreak. There, Williams uncorked an ace to take a 5-3 lead and eventually finished off the match 7-4 for her first WTA Tour title. And to make things even better, older sister Venus won her event in Oklahoma City hours later to mark the first time siblings won on the same weekend on the WTA Tour.

"I've always dreamed of winning Grand Slams, and this is a start," Serena said. "It's good to win a smaller tournament because when I get to the big events, I will have the experience."[54]

Williams still did not have enough WTA Tour points to be seeded at the Evert Cup the following week, but that failed to slow her down. Feeling fully confident after her victory in Paris, she followed it up with her first Tier I WTA title at Indian Wells. Williams upset the second-seeded Davenport in the second round, No. 6 seed Pierce in the quarterfinals, and ousted 12th-seeded Testud in the semis.[55]

Williams would get another crack at Graf, the flag-bearer of the sport with 21 Grand Slam titles among her staggering 106 WTA Tour titles to her credit. Graf was also the two-time defending champion at Indian Wells, but the precocious 17-year-old was more than willing to rally from the baseline with the woman nicknamed "Fraulein Forehand."

Like her previous final in Paris, Williams grabbed the first set before the more experienced Graf found her groove to force a decisive third. Graf broke Williams in the first game of the third set, but her younger opponent refused to relent and continued attacking with her forehand. It eventually paid off with a break in the eighth game, and Williams did so again with Graf serving to extend the match to a tiebreaker at 5-6. After a forehand by Graf had sailed long, Williams became the first player to beat the German in a final since the 1994 U.S. Open.[56]

Williams carried her 11-match win streak to Miami where she was seeded 16th for the Lipton Championships. Often considered the fifth major because of its 96-strong field, she was in a 12-person field of the tournament that was highlighted by third-seeded Monica Seles.

Williams continued her excellent play and rolled past Seles in the fourth round, dropping just five games as she ran her winning streak to 14 matches.

After easing by Amanda Coetzer in the quarterfinals, Williams would face Hingis for the second time in Key Biscayne in as many years, just one round deeper this time. For her part, Hingis was eager for a rematch after last year's encounter, saying "I'd love to play against Serena again. I think everybody has improved since last year."[57]

Indeed. This time, Williams got the better of Hingis by a 6-4, 7-6 (7-3) count, setting up a final against defending champion and elder sister Venus. Serena Williams had to dig out of an early 4-0 hole and staved off a set point in the second set down 5-2 to overcome 49 errors, pounding out 48 winners to defeat the Swiss star.[58] Venus, meanwhile, needed three sets to eliminate Graf.

Unlike previous meetings between the two at the professional level, this was the first time the siblings would be competing in the finals of a tournament on the WTA Tour. It also prompted some feverish research by the WTA, who determined the last pair of female siblings to contest a final were Maud and Lillian Watson at Wimbledon in 1884.[59]

There was something at stake for both sisters – in Venus' case, it was defending her title and remaining perfect against Serena as a pro. For Serena, that first win over Venus would not only extend her win streak to 17 matches and give her a third straight title. It would also propel her into the top 10 of the WTA Tour rankings.

Like most of their early games between them, the contest proved to be a case of nerves and jitters. Venus may be the one person who is apparently nonplussed by Serena's power, and the quickness that goes with the older sister's 6-foot-2 frame allows her to track down almost any shot by any player, regardless of force.

Also in Venus' favor is that she serves as hard as Serena. The elder sister controlled the early part of the match and stormed to a 6-1 lead. Finally feeling the fatigue of her grueling yet successful five-week run, the younger Williams made a match of it by taking the second set and drawing even at 4-all in the third before finally running out of gas. Venus broke her younger sister and showed no mercy serving out the match, not giving Serena a point as she improved to 3-0 in the blossoming sibling rivalry.

"Serena always comes back and defeats people, and I didn't want to become another victim," Venus said. "But in the end, we go home; we live life. You have to remind yourself that it's just a game, and there's only one winner.

"I always dreamed of seeing her on the other side of the net, and now that my game is taken to a different level, it's going to happen more," Serena chimed in.

But the bigger winner of the match may have been their father Richard, who was more than happy to waive the rule regarding trophies won by either of his daughters in the house given the historic event that took place.[60]

Serena Williams took a deserved five-week break after the Lipton Championships to recharge ahead of the French Open. She returned to action in Rome for a clay-court tune-up and lost to Hingis in the quarterfinals, which was a defeat Venus avenged with a victory in the semis. An injury forced Serena to retire in the second set of the quarterfinals of the German Open against Arantxa Sanchez Vicario.

The French Open proved to be a disappointment as Williams lost to American compatriot Mary Joe Fernandez in the third round in three sets. Williams committed 42 unforced errors and incurred the wrath of the crowd by taking out her frustrations on the chair with her racket. Fernandez, who reached the final of the 1993 French Open, played a masterful game of mixing paces and shots, flustering the teenager.

"There was no excuse for the way I played today, really," Williams said. "I should have been taken off the court and immediately asked to leave the facilities, never to return again."[37]

Despite her struggles on the clay at Roland Garros in singles, she and Venus teamed up to win the doubles title at the French Open, their first as partners. Serena was forced to miss Wimbledon due to injury, but did make her Fed Cup debut for the U.S. later that summer and routed Italy's Rita Grande in the semifinals.[62]

She made her return three weeks later near her Compton home in Los Angeles at the Acura Classic. After surviving a first-round scare and rallying past Likhovtseva in three sets, Williams did not drop a set the rest of the way en route to her third title of the year. She topped Sanchez Vicario in the quarterfinals and Hingis in the semis before defeating Halard-Decugis in the final.[63]

That would serve as her last tune-up before finally breaking through on the biggest stage – the U.S. Open.

Chapter 4: First Grand Slam Title at the 1999 U.S. Open

Williams was the No. 7 seed at Flushing Meadows in a field that featured previous champions Hingis, Davenport – the defending title-holder – and Sanchez Vicario. Graf had retired 17 days before the start of the U.S. Open, with the five-time winner's absence leaving a gaping hole in the field.[64] Williams was also in the bottom half of the draw, which meant the only chance of facing her older sister would be in the final.

The younger Williams started with purpose, dropping just one game to Po in the first round. She then eased by Jelena Kostanic in the second round, setting up an intriguing encounter with Belgian teenager Kim Clijsters in the round of 32. Clijsters had made a name for herself in Wimbledon earlier that year, qualifying and eventually reaching the fourth round before losing to Graf.

And unlike the first two opponents, Clijsters was not going to roll over. In fact, she took the first set from Williams only to have the American find her groove in the second to square the match. This is where Williams' big match experience gained earlier in the season during her winning streak proved highly valuable as Clijsters pulled ahead 5-2 in the third set and still served for the match at 5-3.

Williams, though, went for broke and turned the tide. She won 16 of the last 17 points of that match for a wild three-set victory punctuated by a jump and a scream after Clijsters sailed a forehand wide after scrambling to return a shot.[65] When the two met again at the U.S. Open 10 years later in 2009, after Clijsters had come out of retirement, she recalled the moment like it had just happened, noting that "she just, bang, started going for aces, started hitting winners. Like something switched in her head."[66]

The slow starts would occur in each of the next two matches, forcing Williams to rally past 16th-seeded Conchita Martinez in the fourth round and then No. 4 seed Seles in the quarterfinals. In the semifinals against the defending champion Davenport, Williams was the one who grabbed the early advantage only to see Davenport raise her game to take the second set as the two mirrored each other with booming serves and big forehands.

Williams' serve, however, outlasted Davenport's as she went up a break in the third set. Davenport extended the contest by staving off two match points down 5-3, but Serena calmly held serve and advanced to her first Grand Slam final after a backhand by Davenport sailed long.[67]

On the other side of the draw, Hingis rolled through her first five matches without dropping a set before facing Venus Williams in the semifinals. There, she thwarted Richard Williams' dream of seeing his daughters face off in the U.S. Open final as he predicted at the start of the tournament with a gritty three-set victory.

This was the latest flash point over the fortnight in New York. It was now clear that Hingis did not care for either Williams sister as they emerged as viable threats to her No. 1 world ranking. Nor did she care much for their father predicting an all-Williams final, reacting to the comment with usual frankness before her first match: Hingis said the Williams family had "a big mouth" and then added, "They always talk a lot. It's more pressure on them. Whether they can handle it or not, now that's the question."

The younger Williams took a shot at Hingis' lack of formal education, which was somewhat surprising considering both she and Venus were home-schooled at the choice of their father.

"She's always been the type of person that … says things, just speaks her mind," Serena said. "I guess it has a little bit to do with not having a formal education. But you just have to somehow think more; you have to use your brain a little more in the tennis world.

"Obviously she's no. 1, so she can say whatever she would like to say. I personally don't think my mouth is big, if you're just looking at it."[68]

Hingis, who had denied Venus Williams the family's first Grand Slam singles title at the 1997 U.S. Open, was in her third Grand Slam final of 1999. She won the Australian Open, but had melted down against Graf at Roland Garros before a stunning first-round flop at Wimbledon. But she was still the world's top-ranked player and looking for her seventh overall Slam title.

There was also some history the younger Williams was trying to achieve as she looked to become the first female African-American player in the Open Era to win a Grand Slam title and the first since Althea Gibson successfully defended her title at the 1958 U.S. Open.

And, of course, they were playing in the stadium named after Arthur Ashe, the pioneer of African-American tennis on the men's side. He was the last African-American player of either gender to win the U.S. Open in 1968 as well as the last African-American to win a Grand Slam singles title at Wimbledon in 1975.[69]

Williams started out of the gate fast, breaking Hingis on her first service of the game with a thunderous forehand that clipped the baseline for a 2-0 lead. At one point, she fired an ace at 108 mph down the middle that Hingis could not touch as the two held serve the next two games.

Despite her deft play and mixes of shots and angles, it was apparent that Hingis' semifinal victory over Venus Williams had created residual fatigue in the final against Serena. Hingis did not lack for break point opportunities. She had one in every game Serena Williams served in the first set, but Williams' big serve often allowed her to escape unscathed.

Williams was clearly the aggressor in the match. At one point in the first set, she had 13 winners to Hingis' one, but she also had made 16 unforced errors to the Swiss star's three. Williams converted a break point up 4-3 when she rifled a two-handed backhand up the line, and then held serve to win the first set, getting the last two points with an ace and a service winner.

Williams gained a break early in the second set, but Hingis returned the set to serve when she broke back to make it 3-3. Williams did not let it faze her in the next game, ripping a cross-court winner to start and earning three break points after Hingis pushed a backhand wide at love-30.

Hingis saved the first two break points, but Williams forced Hingis wide with a forehand before delivering an unreturnable two-handed backhand to the other side for a 4-3 lead.[70]

She had to work to consolidate the break in the next game, originally squandering it at 40-30 when she netted a backhand with Hingis out of position. But she quickly won the next two points to move to one game from winning the U.S. Open. The next game started favorably for Williams as Hingis picked a most inopportune time for her first double fault of the match.[71]

Williams made it 15-30 when she pounced on a second serve and pulled a backhand winner down the line. She gained two championship points after hitting an off-balance cross-court winner but let the first one get away with a backhand that went wide. Williams then netted a forehand to return the game to deuce, and the jitters of having the match in her hands became apparent as she hit a long forehand while flat-footed.

Hingis hit a forehand long to bring it back to deuce again, but Williams netted a backhand. Hingis finally extended the match after Williams hit a forehand wide to make it 4-5, but Williams could still win the match if she held serve.

But a first anything at the highest levels of sport, let alone a first Grand Slam title, rarely come easy, and such was the case here. First came a backhand that went long, then a backhand into the net. Hingis was content to simply extend rallies and let Williams make the mistakes for points. It went to love-40 after Williams hit a forehand that just missed clipping the baseline.[72]

After Williams sailed a forehand long that was arguably her worst unforced error of the match to that point, the second set was now 5-all. The match was swinging in Hingis' favor as a worldwide audience watched Williams try to deal with the pressure that comes with winning a first Grand Slam title.

Even at the age of 18, Hingis showed a playing maturity that belied her age. Williams launched another forehand long as her footwork deserted her. Hingis was not registering any aces, but her service placement handcuffed Williams on multiple occasions and a netted backhand resulted in an eighth straight point for Hingis and a 30-love lead.

Williams finally ended the run with a forehand winner that kissed the line, and she drew even at 30-all after a Hingis forehand lob landed long. The two traded points to get to deuce, but Williams netted yet another backhand and hit a second one long as Hingis took a 6-5 lead and was four points from forcing a third set.[73]

Williams had made 12 unforced errors in the last three games and added a 13th to start the 12th game of the set when she mishit a backhand. Then the hole got deeper as she double-faulted to make it love-30.

On the next point, Williams forced Hingis wide with her serve, but on the return, Williams was surprised by the amount of topspin Hingis generated and was too tight on the ball. The result was Williams hitting an odd-looking backhand that lazily fell into the frontcourt. Hingis could not get to it in time, and that innocent-looking point proved to be enough of a momentum stopper to let Williams regroup.[74]

On her second serve on the next point, Williams caught a break when Hingis hit a backhand that clipped the net and set up a high bounce. That allowed Williams to charge the net and stab a backhand on a passing shot to level the game at 30-all. Hingis made a rare charge to the net on the next point as she got to a drop shot, only to have Williams launch a perfectly placed lob over her that hit the baseline to make it 40-30. Williams herself smiled in disbelief at the point, knowing that she could not have placed the shot any better with any less margin of error.[75]

Hingis gathered her bearings and forced deuce with a well-placed forehand, and the two would go to a second deuce after Williams narrowly missed a backhand long. Hingis gained a break point when Williams netted a backhand, but the Swiss star finally cracked and netted a weak forehand.[76] Hingis then pulled a forehand wide, but recovered to force a fourth deuce with a forehand winner down the line.

Williams pushed Hingis wide to set up another game point, but squandered it when she netted a forehand with the whole court open to her.[77] After Hingis hit a backland long, Williams finally sent the second set into a tiebreaker when she raced in to pummel a backhand past Hingis, who charged the net after a previous Williams' shot clipped the net and tried a deft cross-court backhand into the forecourt.[78]

Williams had the better tiebreak statistics that year, winning all five of hers while Hingis had split eight previous ones. But then again, none of the previous five had a U.S. Open championship riding on them. By this point, Williams knew Hingis could not overpower her even on her first service and was in front of the baseline to return them. But Williams also continued to battle her nerves as she sent a backhand wide on the first point.

She found her composure on serve, getting both points and cracking a service winner down the middle to go up 2-1. Williams went up a mini-break when Hingis sailed a forehand long, but Hingis won the next point. Williams restored her two-point lead before the changeover when Hingis' service return went long, but Hingis got the tiebreak back on serve when Williams sent a forehand too deep.

Hingis pulled even at 4-4 after Williams netted a forehand to end a grueling baseline rally, but Williams took full advantage of Hingis' soft second serve, smacking a forehand winner to get a second mini-break that also gave her a chance to serve out for the championship.[79]

Williams earned a third championship point when Hingis audaciously tried a lob that went barely long. And after a short rally ended with Hingis sending a forehand long down the middle, Serena Williams had earned her first Grand Slam title, making history as the first African-American to win a Grand Slam title in nearly a quarter-century and the first African-American female to accomplish the feat in over 40 years.[80]

She had a look of disbelief at first before finally beginning to celebrate as she walked to the net to accept a handshake from Hingis. Her parents Richard and Oracene were celebrating, and her sister Venus, watching quietly away from her parents in the same box with a black hoodie, did likewise. Serena then made her way over to where her parents were and climbed the wall to get a hug from her mother.[81] She also got a hug from her father before accepting the trophy, and realized afterward that she had become a champion by playing like one when facing adversity.

"I think after I lost those two match points, I was very upset with myself," Williams said. "I thought for sure I was going to hold my serve at 5-4. I guess something went dreadfully wrong. There comes a time when you just have to stop caving. In the end, I told myself, 'You're going to have to perform.' That's what I did."[82]

One of the perks of the title was a phone call from then-President Clinton, though Williams also found time for a brief conversation with his daughter Chelsea.[83] A footnote to the tournament is that a day later, she and Venus won the Women's Doubles title for their second Grand Slam title of the year.

Women's tennis was about to enter a whole new era on many fronts. One of the false ones, though, was the belief that the rivalry between Hingis and Serena Williams would carry on for years. The matches that the two teenagers played throughout 1999 gave every indication that would be the case, and it had the potential of a rivalry heightened by their highly contrasting personalities.

But that would be the last U.S. Open final Hingis would play. She would be forced to retire at the age of 22 due to a series of hip and ankle injuries. While she would make a series of comebacks in singles, Hingis found more success in doubles in the later stages of her career, winning four Grand Slam titles since the start of 2015 and 12 overall to go with her five Grand Slam singles titles.

Williams' triumph raised the profile of women's tennis and gave women's sports another boost in terms of publicity and marketability. It came barely two months after the U.S. National Team won the Women's World Cup in soccer, beating China in penalty kicks in a sold-out Rose Bowl in Pasadena, California. Both Williams and the U.S. Women's Soccer team would have plenty of staying power over the next generation, but it turned out Williams' reign in her sport as an individual would outlast the national team at the world level.

Chapter 5: Dominance that Spans Decades

Williams played only two more tournaments for the rest of 1999, winning the Grand Slam Cup in Munich at the end of September. She got her first professional win over her older sister in the final, defeating Venus in three sets. Serena started fast, limiting her older sister to just three points in the first five games while winning the first set 6-1. Venus, however, would recover to take the second set by a 6-3 count before Serena regrouped for her first win in four tries for family bragging rights.[84]

Not that you could have guessed from Serena that she won bragging rights after the match. Unlike the previous matches between the two that would often have both sisters battling nerves as much as each other at points, this was a high-powered tennis match that drained both of them. And it was evident that it took a toll on the younger Williams.

"I'd never actually beaten Venus; I didn't know how it feels," Serena said. "It's kind of tough to take this win."[85]

She completed her season at the Porsche Tennis Grand Prix the following week, losing to Testud in three sets in a round of 16 match.[86] But the younger Williams was named the Most Improved Player on the WTA Tour for the year and finished as the No. 4 ranked player in the world.

2000

Williams opted to play in the Australian Open as her first tournament of the year and entered Melbourne as the No. 3 seed. She had to adjust to being the focus of opponents as opposed to being able to sneak up on them as an underdog. Williams had to slug her way past wild-card and local favorite Andrea Grahame in three sets in the first round.[87]

Things went back to normal for the next two rounds as Williams posted straight-set wins over Nicole Pratt and Sabine Appelmans, but her fourth-round match against the 16th-seeded Likhovtseva was a disaster. Whether it was a lack of match fitness after not playing for three months or just a bad day on the court, Williams sprayed shots everywhere as her backhand failed her and she made 32 unforced errors.[88]

She led 3-1 in the first set before Likhovtseva reeled off eight straight wins bridging the two sets. Williams rallied to tie the second set at 3-all, but the Russian regrouped to close out the match.

"I couldn't make any shots ... I couldn't do anything," Williams said. "There's no excuse for me to have lost this match. I just couldn't find my rhythm throughout the whole match."[89]

She returned to Paris at the Open de Gaz as a defending champion for the first time and was almost successful, losing to Tauziat in straight sets in the final. That motivated her enough to claim her first title of the year in Hanover, Germany, where she won the Faber Grand Prix with an emphatic 6-1, 6-1 rout of Denisa Chladkova.[90]

There were high-profile tournaments to defend in the United States at both Indian Wells and Miami, but Williams was unable to string together enough good performances at either to do so. She needed three sets to win her first two matches at Indian Wells before beating Clijsters to reach the quarterfinals, but Pierce proved to be too good as Williams took just three games from the American playing out of France.

In Florida, she was sent packing a round earlier as Capriati, now in the midst of a personal and professional resurgence on the WTA Tour, eliminated her in a three-set match.[91]

In her next tournament at Amelia Island, Williams was forced to retire in the second round of her match against Argentina's Paola Suarez due to a knee injury. Williams had previously dealt with tendinitis at this time last year, and the injury proved to be a repeat of that condition.[92] Taking no chances at such an early point in her career,

Williams opted to skip the clay-court season, which meant no European tournaments or French Open in 2000.

After what turned out to be her second three-month layoff in less than a calendar year, Williams returned to action at Wimbledon where she was the eighth seed. Fully healthy in both body and mind, she plowed through her first five opponents, not dropping a set and losing only 13 games in those ten sets.

In the semifinals, though, her elder sister loomed. Venus Williams was still looking for her first Grand Slam singles title and had not been to a final since losing to Hingis in the 1997 U.S. Open. It once again brought back the talking point of the Watson sisters meeting at Wimbledon in 1884 because now a spot in a Grand Slam final was at stake.

Regarding aesthetics, the match proved to be a letdown as the sisters appeared tentative and skittish. Both of them never truly found a rhythm, but Serena Williams was overwhelmed by the moment and was spraying unforced errors all over the court. Neither played the serve-and-volley game that rewards good players at Wimbledon and were content to try and outslug each other from the baseline, but the younger Williams simply could not get it together.

The result was a 6-2, 7-6 (7-3) victory for the older sister that left Serena inconsolable afterward. After the match had ended with her sixth double fault, the younger Williams cried on the sideline and was still in tears in the post-match interview room.[93]

"I just didn't play well today; it just didn't go right for me," she said. "Venus played pretty well today and she brought out her best game against me, and I guess I wasn't all that ready. I expected to play a lot better today. It was my goal to do better. I'm only 18; Venus is 20. I got a lot of years ahead of me."[94]

The way the match unfolded also marked the first time the sisters would be dogged by the idea of possible "match-fixing" in which the sisters, in tandem with their father, would choose who would win a given tournament. Richard Williams, who did not even attend the match and was walking around the nearby streets of the all-England club because he was so nervous, dismissed such a notion while Venus gave a sharp, "No, not that I'm aware of," reply to the question.[95]

If there was a silver lining to such a horrid match, it was that the sisters captured their third doubles Grand Slam title at Wimbledon with a straight-set win over Halard-Decugis and Japan's Ai Sugiyama.

Serena Williams stayed away from tennis until the start of August, but her older sister was dominating tournaments and headlines with victories in Stanford and San Diego. The younger Williams returned to defend her title at Manhattan Beach, and for one tournament at least, everything clicked.

She rolled through her first two matches and worked hard in the last three, needing three sets from the quarterfinals forward. Williams knocked off No. 4 seed Conchita Martinez before rallying past the top-seeded Hingis in the semifinals. The final against Davenport featured wild swings of brilliant and erratic tennis as the two battled in the sweltering heat as the temperature climbed above 90 degrees.[96]

There was only one break in the first set, which Davenport capitalized on to win 6-4. The two traded breaks five times in the second as Williams leveled the match, and then the two broke the other's serve three times in the decisive third set. Williams, though, claimed the most important one as she broke Davenport at love trailing 6-5 to force a tiebreaker. After the two had split the first two points, Williams won the final six points of the 2-hour, 28-minute match that featured a total of 21 double faults by the two players.[97]

The injury bug bit Williams for a second time in 2000, this time in the final of the du Maurier Classic in Montreal. She was trailing Hingis 3-0 in the third set before complaining of pain in her left foot.[98] It would not derail her from attempting to defend her U.S. Open title where Hingis would again be the top seed and Williams was seeded fifth.

Much like Wimbledon, Williams was impressive in the early rounds, getting four wins without dropping a set and being pushed to a tiebreak just once in those eight sets. In the quarterfinals, though, the second-seeded Davenport avenged her loss in Los Angeles with a thorough 6-4, 6-2 pasting of Williams.

Davenport had won just one of the previous six matches between the two, but she used the unorthodox strategy of repeatedly pumping shots into a corner to force Williams to lose her patience in returning them.[99] She also got a boost of confidence early in the match by fending off three break points for Williams, whose impatience hastened her demise. Davenport made the most of her one break point in the first set and then tired out Williams by making her save five match points at 5-1 in the second.

"The difference was Lindsay just played better than I did," Williams said. "You can't afford to be on anything but your best game in the quarterfinals of a Grand Slam."[100]

She did not qualify for singles at the Sydney Olympics because Davenport and her sister were the two highest-ranked American players, but she did team up with Venus to win a gold medal in women's doubles, routing the Dutch tandem of Kristie Boogert and Miriam Oremans 6-1, 6-1. It extended their winning streak to 22 matches, and for Serena, she was a happy cheerleader for her big sister as she won the gold in singles the day before.[101]

"It was a happy moment for me Wednesday, watching Venus win," Serena said. "It was the same kind of feeling today."[102]

The younger Williams capped her season with a title at the Toyota Princess Cup in Tokyo before she and Venus took off the rest of the year to do academic work.[103] All told, it was a successful year for Serena as she finished with three titles and a world ranking of No. 6, though that drop of two spots could be attributed to the lack of tournaments she played due to injury.

2001

It was an impressive climb by Williams to her thoroughly entrenched Top 10 status, but getting to that upper echelon and breaking into the top 5 where her sister resided continued to be a formidable challenge. This time, she entered a tournament in Sydney to prepare for the Australian Open, and Hingis bounced her in the quarterfinals.[104]

The scenario would play out again in Melbourne as the "Swiss Miss" avenged her U.S. Open finals defeat with a contentious three-set victory. Hingis won the first set, and Williams called for the trainer when she felt light-headed. After receiving fluids and "some pink stuff" Williams said tasted "terrible," she roared back to take the second.

The third set was riveting, with Williams racing ahead 4-1 only to have Hingis break her twice around fending off four break points of her own to level the match. Williams answered with a break of her own and was two points from closing out the match on serve before Hingis again responded to the challenge and would eventually win the third set 8-6.[105]

After the match, Williams claimed she had an upset stomach and had barely eaten anything over the previous two days, but Hingis was not buying any of it in the post-match interview.

"You couldn't really tell that she had food poisoning or anything," said Hingis, who said her first-set play was the best of her career.

"She was running well. When she lost in some of the long rallies, it was more that I wore her out, not that there was anything else you could see was the problem."[106]

There may have been some truth to those words considering that barely an hour after the defeat, Williams was able to win a three-set doubles match with her sister. The other truth is that Williams did not help herself much by committing 54 unforced errors compared to only 29 by Hingis.[107]

Williams did not play again until Indian Wells, a tournament that is forever remembered in women's tennis for all the wrong reasons. It started normal enough, with Williams seeded seventh and having little trouble navigating the field. She did not drop a set in her first three matches and routed Davenport 6-1, 6-2 in the quarterfinals to set up a semifinal against her sister.

After Venus Williams had defeated Elena Dementieva in the quarterfinals, the Russian raised some eyebrows in her post-match interview by stating that she felt Richard Williams had already determined who was going to advance to the finals. When asked directly if other players felt that way, Dementieva said "no" and that she "didn't talk about it with the other players."[108]

Without directly saying it was fixed, Dementieva also felt that the 1999 final in Miami had a pre-arranged outcome, noting that, "if you saw this match, it was so funny." In this instance, the WTA failed to help matters by not releasing any follow-up statement to Dementieva's comments.[109]

The next problem came the day of the semifinals when Venus pulled out just minutes before the scheduled start time of the match due to a knee injury. The timing is important to note in this instance because players are advised to give at least 30 minutes' notice so tournament officials can reschedule the match order and such. As a result, tournament director Charlie Pasarell only learned of Venus' withdrawal via the PA system at the court. His words also failed to help matters:

"I only wish she had gone out and given it a try. This hurts the game of tennis more than the individual tournament."[110]

This statement, coupled with how both Richard Williams and the sisters dealt with the media with regards to possible match-fixing, now stirred the public's imagination. During the week, *The National Enquirer* ran a story claiming that two sources close to Richard Williams had told Serena to lose to Venus in the Wimbledon final the previous year.[111]

In the interviews after the match that never took place, neither sister came out with an outright denial that any match was fixed or that their father pre-arranged any outcome in a game between the two of them. If anything, Serena added further controversy by saying, "I think maybe if my dad did decide, then maybe Venus wouldn't be up 4-1, maybe it would be three-all by now."[112]

The following day, the WTA finally put out a statement saying that "they were aware of the assertions being circulated regarding Venus and Serena Williams' head-to-head matches." But they also stated that they found no evidence of wrongdoing and that both players denied any such assertions.[113] However, the mushroom cloud from this whole affair was still growing, and it got even worse the next day.

While Serena was taking warm-ups for her final against Clijsters, both Richard and Venus Williams made their way to their seats. Although accounts from various media members differ in some respects, one common thread existed: both of them were booed loudly by the sellout crowd of nearly 16,000. It continued throughout the match, and at one point before the match started, Richard Williams shook his fist at the crowd.[114]

There were no physical incidents, and tournament officials did not report any racial abuse hurled at either Richard or Venus, though security did eventually sit by them during the match, which was won by Serena in three sets.[115] The real fallout, though, came nine days later when Richard Williams told USA Today that "When Venus and I were walking down to our seats, people kept calling me 'n-----.' One said, 'I wish it was '75, we'd skin you alive.' I think Indian Wells disgraced America."[116]

Pasarell was also quoted in that story, saying, "I was cringing when all that stuff was going on. It was unfair for the crowd to do that."[117]

The sisters tried their best to deal with the questions of racism asked of them ahead of their next tournament in Miami, but remember, Venus was still only 20 and Serena just 19. Venus tried her best to sidestep the question but also noted that "Whatever happened, happened. I can't change it. There's nothing I can do about it."[118]

Serena claimed that her father did not tell her about the comments he made to USA Today and also said that it was probably in her best interests because "maybe I would have been a little more emotional about it."[119] A full two weeks after the whole incident started with off-hand remarks by Dementieva, she said at a press conference in Miami that "she was kidding" and "didn't think" it would ever get to that level of scrutiny.[120]

In the end, the sisters would start boycotting Indian Wells, which would last until Serena returned to play in 2015. By 2009, the event had become one of four Premier Mandatory events on the WTA Tour that eligible players were required to enter. The tour also said that skipping such an event would warrant a potential suspension unless the player did promotional activities for the event missed.[121] There may or may not have been a distance set of 125 miles as the break-off point since the Williams sisters resided 128 miles from Indian Wells.[122]

Williams did her best to put aside the distractions that Indian Wells created, but she lost to Capriati in the quarterfinals in Miami. She did not play again until the French Open, where Capriati's resurgence continued with a three-set win over Williams in the semifinals.[123] Once both the poster girl and cautionary tale for teenagers in women's tennis but now a wizened 21-year-old, Capriati would go on to claim the title at Roland Garros and rally to defeat Williams once more at Wimbledon in the quarterfinals.

Williams, though, had her chances to win this match and was two points from victory in the second set before Capriati went for broke. Williams dropped nine straight games at one point as Capriati finished off a three-set win by a 6-7 (4-7), 7-5, 6-3 scoreline.[124] Williams twice dealt with an upset stomach in both the first and third sets, and nearly rallied after the second instance as she won three straight games to close within 4-3 before faltering.

Williams claimed post-match that she had barely eaten for four days, but her reputation was already chastened from the Hingis match in Melbourne as well as the whole saga at Indian Wells, and Capriati was simply the next in line to call out what she thought was poor sportsmanship by Williams.

"It doesn't matter," said Capriati, who received treatment for a hip injury while Williams had her first bout with her stomach disorder. "I think I know the truth inside. I think most people do. ... I mean, it's pretty much the same things that happen every time I play her. So I'm used to that."[125]

Williams would eventually get her first tournament win of the year in Toronto, navigating a difficult path that saw her defeat four seeded players to finally get the better of Capriati in a three-set final. That was her tune-up to the U.S. Open where her year-long slump had dropped her to a 10th seed.

The confidence from Toronto carried over to Flushing Meadow, though she did have a first-round scare against Anca Barna in dropping the first set. Williams lost just three games in winning her next two matches before beating Justine Henin to reach the quarterfinals. There, she outlasted Davenport in three sets before mowing down the top-seeded Hingis 6-3, 6-2.[126]

Her opponent in the finals would be her sister and defending champion, Venus. Unlike Indian Wells in February, which was a disaster for all involved, this turned out to be another essential touchstone in the growth of both women's tennis and women's sports. And once more, the sports media would trot out the 1884 Wimbledon final between the Watson sisters as the last previous time siblings met in a Grand Slam final.

Before the tournament, United States television rights holder CBS announced the women's final would be played in prime time on Saturday night because of the surge in popularity in the game. That was primarily due to the Williams sisters, but also in part due to Capriati's standout play that year and the ongoing rivalry the sisters had with Hingis.[127]

The issue of racism was again brought to the forefront by Hingis, who was still the world's No. 1 player at the time. In the issue of Time

Magazine that coincided with the start of the U.S. Open, Hingis claimed that the Williams sisters "get sponsors because they are black and have lots of advantages because they can always say it's racism."[128]

Serena Williams blasted back at the comments after her first-round win, saying, "I wouldn't know anything about getting endorsements because I am black. I get them because I win and work hard."[129]

The match itself played out once more as it had for most of the previous five when the sisters have met. On one side was Venus, showing poise and looking for the sliver of weakness the overeager and overaggressive Serena could make over the course of a point and, more often than not, exploiting it.

Serena is always going to be the more aggressive of the two players, but more often than not, it plays right into Venus' style of play. And however hard Serena hits the ball, Venus has the power to return it along with the consistency her younger sister still had not found by the sixth professional match between the two.

So once more it was Venus emerging victorious, this time in an efficient 6-2, 6-4 scoreline. What the match lacked in riveting tennis it more than compensated for by its status as stand-alone prime-time sports programming on a Saturday night in the United States. The biggest confirmation of that came from another of women's tennis original pioneers, Billie Jean King. She was part of one of tennis' biggest prime-time moments, her "Battle of the Sexes" victory over Bobby Riggs in the Houston Astrodome in 1973.

"I think this night is another moment to cherish," said King, who was one of the nine founding players of the WTA Tour in 1971. "Serena and Venus are providing another benchmark for women's sports. I was thinking about 1973 and how women couldn't even get a credit card back then."[130]

She jokingly added, "Can you imagine Serena and Venus without a credit card?"[131]

Serena Williams ended her season on a positive note by winning the season-ending Sanex WTA Championship in Munich. She was awarded the title when Davenport was unable to play due to a knee injury suffered in her semifinal win over Clijsters.[132] Williams would be ranked sixth at year's end for the second straight season.

2002

Now well into her career, Williams had generated more controversy than championships, especially when it came to Grand Slam singles titles. People kept waiting for her to break through to that upper echelon, something that can be argued Serena herself was impatiently trying to achieve. It would finally take place in 2002.

The season, though, started on an ominous note. Williams sprained her ankle in the first set of her semifinal in Sydney against Meghann Shaughnessy and was forced to retire. She withdrew from the

Australian Open before the start of the tournament because she was unable to have full range of motion in practices leading up to the first Grand Slam of the year.[133]

"It's tough because, as a competitor, I've set my goals a bit higher this year," Williams said. "It's a hardcourt. I love hardcourts, and to be quite honest with you, the last few tournaments, I've been really positive. I think I could have done beyond well."[134]

Williams would miss six weeks before making her return to Arizona at the State Farm Women's Tennis Classic. Despite its Tier II status, the tournament drew top names as a tune-up event for Indian Wells, which Williams would not attend. She beat both Hingis and Capriati in three-set matches in the final two rounds to claim her first tournament victory of the year.[135]

Williams then made history at the Miami Masters by becoming the first player to beat the top three players in the world at one tournament. She beat Hingis in the quarterfinals and surprisingly routed her sister in the semis before grinding past Capriati 7-5, 7-6 (7-4) in an error-strewn final. Williams hit 59 of the 97 unforced errors between the two, but she also racked up 31 winners as her aggressive style kept the trophy in the family after Venus had won the previous year.[136]

The clay-court season was a mixed bag for Williams, who was upset in the quarterfinals in Charleston before crossing the Atlantic to play in Europe. There she lost to Henin in the final in Berlin before beating her the following week in Rome as everyone prepped for the French Open.

Williams was seeded third at Roland Garros behind Capriati, the defending champion, and her older sister. She dropped just 12 games in rolling through her first three matches before encountering her first obstacle in Russian qualifier Vera Zvonareva.[137] Williams dropped the first set but roared back by losing only one game in winning the next two sets.[138]

Up next was Pierce, who made a surprising run as a wild card and would have the Roland crowd on her side since the American made France her home. Williams, though, needed just 49 minutes to send Pierce packing as she dropped just two games and a mere two points in her final five service games.[139]

Williams would face Capriati in the semifinals as their rivalry continued into a second straight year. After the two Grand Slam losses to Capriati, Williams gained the early upper hand in 2002 by winning all three meetings between them. The two traded breaks throughout the first set, six times in all before Capriati took a 5-3 lead en route to winning the first set.

Williams squandered a 5-2 lead in the second set and was dragged into a tiebreaker, but rediscovered her form to force the third set. There, Williams' powerful serve proved to be the difference as she finally ended her Slam struggles against Capriati and set up another Grand Slam finals encounter with her older sister.[140]

As had always been the case previously, the two sisters were skittish against each other and took advantage of poor service games on both ends. Venus fell behind 2-0 early, but won the next four games. The counterpunching game Venus had consistently relied on against her younger sister finally failed to deliver the points she grew accustomed to winning as Serena rallied to take the first set.

The early part of the second set saw Serena take control of the match by going ahead 3-0, though Venus made one last charge to draw within 4-3. Serena, though, held serve on the next game and then broke her older sister, one of 13 in the 21 games played in the match, to claim her second Grand Slam title and arguably her most important win over her older sister to date.[141]

There was the same subdued reaction of celebration by Serena that Venus had done all those times in her previous victories, and Serena addressed Venus in the post-match conference by thanking her "for supporting me the whole way and being the best sister in the whole world."[142]

They had now won six of the last 11 Grand Slam titles between them as the landscape of women's tennis was again changing. It was slowly becoming the Williams sisters against the world as 21 of the final 32 players left in the women's draw were from Europe.[143]

Serena Williams would bypass the grass court season and not play again until Wimbledon. Here, she was seeded second behind her sister and tore through most of the competition. In fact, her toughest match en route to the finals was Belgian qualifier Els Callens, and the 119th-ranked player in the world pushed her to tiebreakers in both sets.[144] The younger Williams, however, quickly restored order as she lost a combined eight games in wins over Daniela Hantuchova and Mauresmo to reach the finals opposite her older sister once more.[145]

Venus Williams had dropped only one set in her six wins, quickly rallying past Canadian Maureen Drake in the third round. But in the span of a year since her quarterfinal loss to Capriati at the All-England club, her younger sister appeared ready to accept all the trappings that came with being an elite player on the world's stage. After beating Venus in Roland Garros, the pace of the pendulum that held sway with her older sister for so long was officially coming Serena's way.

And for the public who yearned for a high-quality match between the sisters, they finally got it in the first set. Though Venus struggled with a shoulder injury that hampered her powerful serve, they engaged in a tense first set in which Serena unleashed a barrage of forehands that Venus deftly defended in a myriad of ways. The younger sister pulled ahead 5-3 only to have Venus bring the match back on serve two games later.[146]

The match swung Serena's way in the tiebreak when she unleashed a blistering forehand for a 3-1 advantage that Venus never overcame. That momentum carried into the second set as Serena continued her hammering of Venus with forehands and powerful serves. It eventually paid off in a break in the eighth game that provided a 5-3 lead. Serena then closed out the match in devastating form, firing three service winners for her second consecutive Grand Slam. She became the first player since Graf in 1996 to win both the French Open and Wimbledon in the same year.[147]

Ranked No. 1 on the WTA Tour for the first time following her Wimbledon title, Serena returned stateside but absorbed just her fifth loss of the calendar year with a quarterfinal defeat to Chanda Rubin in Los Angeles.[148] It would be her only event before the U.S. Open, where she was now top seed and ahead of her defending champion sister.

If there was any doubt about Serena's ascendancy, it would be emphatically vanquished in New York. A pedestrian win over Corina Morariu in the first round was followed with remorseless routs of Dinara Safina, Dechy, Daja Bedanova, and Hantuchova in which she dropped a combined nine games.[149]

Even Davenport, who was still not 100 percent as she was recovering from a knee injury but was still formidable, could not touch her in a 6-3, 7-5 semifinal defeat and acknowledged that Williams was playing at a level no one could match.

"She's played a phenomenal tournament this year," said Davenport, who never shied from giving either sister praise when it was warranted. "She's played a phenomenal three Slams in a row. I mean, that's tough to do."[150]

Once more, it would be Serena vs. Venus in the final of a Grand Slam. Her older sister navigated a tricky path to return to the final, beating Seles and Mauresmo in the quarters and semis, respectively. And the novelty of facing each other in a Grand Slam final had finally worn off to the point that they treated each other as just another opponent between the white lines of the court.

Similar to Wimbledon, there were intense exchanges of powerful forehands and blistering serves in the opening set. At one point, Serena pointed out a shot to the line judge she thought was wide based on the mark of the ball. The two were on level terms until the ninth game, when the younger Williams went up a break after a forehand by Venus went wide. Serena consolidated the break by serving out a love, hammering an ace on set point as an exclamation point.[151]

The second set was more of the same, with Serena finding just enough to answer everything Venus threw at her. Down 5-3, Venus was fighting to extend the match on serve and had calmly turned aside two match points, only to give her sister a third with a double fault. That proved to be one too many as Serena pinned her to the baseline with a corner shot Venus could only hit into the net, and the younger sister not only picked up her third straight Grand Slam title, but also evened the sibling rivalry at 5-5 on the WTA Tour.[152]

"Venus dominated me for a long time, but we always stayed close," Serena said. "Family comes first for us."

What was more telling, though, was Venus' self-professed state of her game. She had gone 0-4 against Serena in 2002 while winning 60 of 63 matches against everyone else. Her father always felt that Serena was the more talented and better long-term player of the two, but the older sister conceded just how much better her younger sibling had become.

"I think my level is about the same" Venus said when asked to compare her play in 2002 to 2001. "Mentally, I'm not there as much. I think Serena's is definitely more up than last year."[153]

Serena Williams would extend her winning streak to 18 matches as she captured titles in Tokyo and Leipzig before losing in the finals of the season-ending Tour Championship to Clijsters. Williams would end the year as the world's top-ranked player and the WTA Tour Player of the Year in 2002. And she had a chance to complete the "Serena Slam" in January in Australia.[154]

2003

The "Serena Slam" was on the minds of everyone who followed tennis as 2003 began. Williams had the chance to hold all four Grand Slam titles simultaneously for the first time in women's tennis since Graf had done so in 1994 and the fifth overall. Additionally, Graf had a "Golden Slam" in 1988 in which she won all four majors in the same calendar year along with an Olympic gold medal. While

Williams could not match that in a non-Olympic year, being Graf's peer at the young age of 21 was still noteworthy.

That quest, however, was nearly derailed right after it began. Playing in a self-designed outfit that could be generously labeled as garish and complete with rhinestones, Williams looked like anything but a four-time Grand Slam winner in the first round against 56th-ranked Emilie Lott of France.[155] At one point, the 23-year-old Lott was just three points from a monumental upset before Williams found her bearings, winning a second-set tiebreak and eventually the match.

While Williams admitted to being "a little nervous and a little tight out there," she insisted not worrying about losing and preferred to focus on her outfit, noting how she used a heat gun to apply the rhinestones.[156]

Williams reasserted her dominance over the next four rounds, winning all of them in straight sets as her Grand Slam winning streak reached 26 matches. Her semifinal match would be against Clijsters, a scrappy fighter who also had the adoration of the Australian Open crowd since she was dating men's tennis star, Lleyton Hewitt.[157] Clijsters and Williams split the first two sets, and Clijsters had a 2-1 lead in the third when Williams took a medical timeout to receive treatment for a blister on her right foot that had burst.

Unfazed by the break, Clijsters ripped off the next three games to take what looked to be an unassailable 5-1 lead. Williams' comeback began modestly by holding serve. She then fought off two match points with the Belgian serving for the match, the second coming on a well-placed forehand that Clijsters could not return.[158]

Once more, Williams held serve to add to the pressure on Clijsters, and here the Belgian waffled. Clijsters double-faulted on the first two points of the game but won the next two. At 30-all, Williams laced a forehand winner and converted the break point when Clijsters made an unforced error on her backhand. Williams would then cap the rally by winning the final two games and keeping alive hopes of the "Serena Slam."

"It was just an unbelievable battle out there," Williams said. "I thought, 'I don't want to lose, 6-1.' Then I said, 'I don't want to lose, 6-2.' So I just kept fighting. Next thing I know, I came back."[159]

The comeback added to the anticipation of the possible completion of the "Serena Slam" since once more it would be Venus in the opposite corner. It would mark the first time in the Open Era, which started in 1968, that two women faced each other in four straight Grand Slam finals. Venus took care of another Belgian in the other semifinal, ousting Justine Henin-Hardenne in straight sets.[160]

This final had a different look early as Venus served notice that she was not going to concede anything. In fact, the older sister had a chance to serve out the first set, but Serena battled back to force a tiebreak that she eventually won 7-4.[161] Determined not to lose a fourth straight Grand Slam final in straight sets, Venus showed championship mettle in forcing a decisive third set.

The two were as scorching as the Australian summer, which had reached 108 degrees and forced officials to put up the cover at the Rod Laver Arena.[162] The third set was punch and counterpunch of the trademark booming serves and powerful forehands that both players were known for. The match progressed beyond two hours as the sisters gave it their all. Venus played a brilliant defensive service game down 4-3, fending off five break points before giving Serena a hard-edged dose of her own medicine with a 120 mile per hour service winner.[163]

That game, though, took enough starch out of Venus that Serena would gain the upper hand. She was able to hold serve for a 5-4 lead, and Venus was her own worst enemy in the final game of the match as she committed three unforced errors and a double fault as her younger sister won her fourth straight Grand Slam title and overtook Venus for career Grand Slam titles with her fifth overall.[164]

"I just can't believe I can now be compared to these great women," said Serena when asked about joining Graf, Navratilova, Margaret Court, and Maureen Connolly as players who held all four titles simultaneously. "They're such greats, and I don't know if I'll ever accomplish everything they have. But to be in the category of winning four in a row for me is really amazing, it's something I've always dreamed of and wanted to do."[165]

Buoyed by her historic victory, Williams had no time for a letdown as she added titles in Paris and Miami to her burgeoning trophy case.

She started the year 21-0 before losing in the finals in Charleston to Henin-Hardenne, but bounced back with a pair of victories in a Fed Cup win for the U.S.[166]

Williams prepped for the French Open by playing in the Rome Masters but lost to Mauresmo in three sets in the semifinals. After winning four straight majors, it was now time for Williams to begin defending each of them, starting at Roland Garros. She was the top seed and played accordingly in winning her first five matches in straight sets, the last a convincing 6-1, 6-2 rout of Mauresmo.[167]

By now, Williams' Grand Slam winning streak had reached 32 matches as she prepared to face Henin-Hardenne. Always ready to root for an underdog, the French Open crowd vociferously backed the Belgian, who played a spirited contest and dogged Williams into some ragged play. The pressure of winning a fifth straight Grand Slam may also have been a factor as the world's top-ranked player repeatedly lost her cool.

The two went into a third set, where the crowd finally turned fully against Williams. Henin-Hardenne hit a shot that was wide but not called out. Williams pointed to the spot in the clay, which is easy to discern given the surface, and the chair umpire agreed, giving Williams the game and a 4-2 lead.[168]

The very next point, the crowd again booed when a ball they thought was good was correctly ruled out to give Williams a 15-love lead. Amidst the din of noise, Henin-Hardenne put her hand up to the umpire to signal for time. Williams did not hear it and smacked a first service into the net. She asked chair umpire Jorge Dias for a second first service, but he refused. Though Williams won that particular point, the crowd had clearly rattled her, and Henin-Hardenne won the next four points for a crucial service break that spurred her to an eventual 6-2, 4-6, 7-5 win.[169]

Williams was upset with the crowd, but also furious with Henin-Hardenne after she denied asking for time. She broke down in tears in the post-match interview, saying the non-call "wasn't the turning point. I probably still should have won the game. But to start lying and fabricating, it's not fair."[170]

She took the customary three-week sojourn from the WTA Tour to recharge for Wimbledon and another Grand Slam title defense. Things went according to plan for the top-seeded Williams as she ran into little difficulty until the quarterfinals against Capriati.[171] What made this match interesting was that if Williams lost, she would also lose her No. 1 world ranking to the hard-charging Clijsters.

Williams was erratic and dropped her first set at Wimbledon since her 2001 quarterfinal defeat to Capriati, but regrouped and forced a decisive third set. She gained control of the match in the first game of the third set, swatting aside two break points en route to a 2-6, 6-2, 6-3 win that marked her eighth straight victory over Capriati.[172]

That win earned her a rematch against Henin-Hardenne, something Williams wanted from the moment she left the Philippe Chatrier center court in Paris. Even with a rain delay that lasted more than two hours, it did not dissipate any of the rage Williams carried into the match. She won the first four games of the match, thumping forehands with menace and malicious intent.[173]

Henin-Hardenne made one brief charge to pull within 4-3, but Williams would entertain no such second acts of a comeback. She closed out the first set and then put away the Belgian with ease for a 6-3, 6-2 win. Revenge sated, the task at hand was adding another Wimbledon title and another match against older sister Venus.

Though the elder Williams had made it back to the Wimbledon final, there was a sense of the six victories being in the Pyrrhic sense. Venus had aggravated an abdominal muscle strain while beating Clijsters and had picked up a hip injury in her last practice session during her fortnight at the all-England Club.[174] Being asked to take down your younger sister, now the better sister, was a tall enough order when fully healthy. Now it bordered on impossible.

It was Venus who was quicker in the early going, breaking Serena in the first game and riding that out to win the first set. Serena answered similarly in the second, and the match was delicately poised between the siblings. Venus, though, finally could not withstand the pain in her injuries in the third set. She had to have her abdomen rewrapped after losing on serve in the first game and never mounted a serious challenge thereafter.[175]

It marked the fourth straight time a Williams sister won the Wimbledon singles title, and it extended Serena's winning streak over Venus to six. But the younger sister felt plenty of empathy as the older one gutted out the match despite her ailments.

"Venus was playing the best the whole tournament," Serena said. "I had to tell myself to look at the ball, nothing else. It's tough. It shows what a great champion Venus is. She's really inspiring for me."[176]

Serena, though, would have to again deal with injury issues of her own. The tendinitis in her left knee had progressed to the point where it partially tore a tendon. Williams had initially committed to play in the three California tournaments before the U.S. Open before having to withdraw from all of them. Now she would not be able to defend her title at Flushing Meadow because she needed surgery.[177]

A promising season was cut short with Williams denied a chance to win three majors for the second straight year. And to add insult to injury, the tournament absences dropped her behind Clijsters for the No. 1 spot on the WTA Tour.

2004

It was initially believed that Williams' knee surgery would cause her to miss only two months, allowing her plenty of time to recover and potentially play in a season-ending tournament or two in 2003 to knock off the layoff-acquired rust. But a personal tragedy befell the

Williams family shortly after Serena's knee surgery: the murder of older half-sister Yetunde Price.

Price, who at times served as a personal assistant to her younger sisters, was shot in her car while with her boyfriend in the family's childhood home of Compton after the two got into an argument with area youths. While Price's boyfriend was unharmed, she was rushed to the hospital and pronounced dead there a short time later.[178]

Williams had been in Toronto for a television appearance filming but quickly changed her plans to reunite with her family in Los Angeles.

"This is extremely devastating news. They are a very close-knit family," wrote Serena's publicist Raymone Bain in a statement to the media.[179]

It would be many years before either sister publicly addressed the impact of Price's murder on their lives. While promoting her 2009 autobiography "On the Line" before the U.S. Open, Williams admitted that she went into a "very dark period" following her half-sister's death and did not open up to anyone in the family, not even her mother, Oracene.[180]

"No one knew I was in therapy, but I was. I was so close to my sister," said Williams, who also estimated she gained at least 15 pounds while battling depression. "It was a real dark period in my life. I never even talked it about with my Mom."[181]

After dropping to sixth in the world, Williams made her eagerly anticipated return to the WTA Tour in Miami in late March of 2014 at the Nasdaq 100. She was the top seed in the tournament, and her eight-month layoff looked more like a mere eight minutes between matches as she thrashed qualifier Marta Marrero 6-1, 6-0 in just 42 minutes in her first game back.[182]

"I definitely knew I had been away," Williams said. "I haven't been around this atmosphere in a long time and felt it. I had a few butterflies at the beginning, but once I stepped on the court, they were gone."[183]

One could have said the same in the competition of a depleted field that was missing Henin-Hardenne, Clijsters, Mauresmo, and Davenport. Still, one can only play who's in front of them, and Williams dropped one set en route to the title and beat a promising young Russian player named Maria Sharapova in straight sets in the third round.[184]

Williams would fail to win any tournaments in her clay-court tune-ups for the French Open, highlighted by a loss to Capriati in the semifinals in Rome. The fiery foil of Williams would claim another win over her at Roland Garros in three sets in the quarterfinals as the two battled during rainy conditions that made the clay even more formidable. That was part of an all-around rough day for the siblings as her older sister Venus was also bounced in the quarterfinals by unheralded Anastasia Myskina.[185]

Serena Williams had now slipped to 10th in the WTA Tour rankings, but she was still the top seed at Wimbledon. And for the first five matches, she looked like the Serena Williams of old as she did not drop a set and routed Capriati 6-1, 6-1 to avenge her French Open defeat from the previous month.[186]

Williams next faced Mauresmo as she bid for her third straight Wimbledon final, and the two put on a brilliant semifinal. They traded breaks in the first set with Mauresmo riding hers to force a tiebreaker that she won.

Williams regrouped in the second set and battled through four consecutive breaks in service of both players until a double fault by Mauresmo gave Williams the second set 7-5. The two continued their high-level play, but it came down to one break of service, which Williams gained to close out the match when Mauresmo hit a forehand wide.[187]

She was now bidding to be the first female player to win three straight Wimbledon titles since Steffi Graf did so from 1991-93 and only the third overall. Her last obstacle was the 13th-seeded Sharapova, a 17-year-old Russian who had never progressed beyond the quarterfinals in her first six Grand Slam appearances.

Sharapova, who had won the Eastbourne tune-up event ahead of Wimbledon, had caught a few breaks on her side of the draw as the No. 2 seed Anastasia Myskina lost in the third round and 3rd-seeded Venus Williams was a second-round upset victim in controversial fashion.[188] Serena Williams rightfully entered the match as an overwhelming favorite, but no one could have predicted the lopsided outcome that was to follow.

Using her full arsenal of shots, the Siberian teenager pulled off a monumental stunner with a 6-1, 6-4 rout of Williams. With nothing to lose, Sharapova threw everything at Williams, and it worked to a shockingly high degree. After they had split the first two games, Sharapova took the next five to win the first set and refused to back down in the second even when Williams broke her for a 4-2 lead.

Sharapova simply regrouped and closed out the match by winning the last four games. Unlike previous Grand Slam defeats where Williams could pick out the point where she lost the match, she was merely second-best to Sharapova on this day.

"It wasn't my day," Serena told the Centre Court crowd. "Maria played a really good match. Congratulations on your first Grand Slam."[189]

Williams slipped as far down as 16th in the WTA rankings, and her title in Beijing would be her only other victory in 2004. Capriati again got the best of her in a Grand Slam event, derailing her bid to repeat as U.S. Open champion in the quarterfinals. But Williams played well enough down the stretch that she re-entered the top 10 in the rankings and qualified for the season-ending Tour Championship.

Sharapova, however, put a bow on her breakout season by defeating Williams in three sets in the final. It had been a draining tournament for Williams, who was forced to decisive third sets in four of the five matches she played.[190]

2005

With the turning of the calendar to a new year, there is always a sense of optimism, and that was no different for Williams after a 2004 to forget. She entered Melbourne as the seventh seed for the Australian Open in her first appearance there since completing the "Serena Slam" in 2003 and was eager to make up for lost time.

She dropped a total of 10 games in rolling through her first three matches before being pushed to three sets by 11th-seeded Nadia Petrova in the fourth round. Williams squared off with No. 2 seed Mauresmo in the quarterfinals but routed the Frenchwoman 6-2, 6-2 for her 12th straight win at the Australian Open.[191]

A spot in the semifinals gave her another crack at Sharapova, whose meteoric rise had landed her a fourth seed. It appeared the Russian would extend her mastery over Williams, winning the first set easily and had a chance to serve out the match at 5-4. But Sharapova's conditioning, which had been an issue in her quarterfinal win over Svetlana Kuznetsova, again came into play in the sweltering Australian sun.[192]

Williams roared back to take the next three games and force a decisive third set. The match swung back and forth, and it was Sharapova again with a chance to close out the match on serve with three match points. Williams defiantly beat each one back with stinging returns to knot the match at 5-all and eventually ousted the Russian teenager by an 8-6 count in the decisive set.[193]

For the first time in six Grand Slam finals Serena reached, Venus would not be her opponent in the final. The older sister, who was seeded eighth, was upended by Australian and 10th seed Alicia Molik in the quarterfinals. Trying to stop Serena from a seventh career Grand Slam title would be the top-seeded Davenport, who needed three sets in both the quarters and semis to advance to her first final since the 2000 US Open.[194]

Despite the taxing route to the finals, it was Davenport who appeared no worse for the wear in the first set. Compounding matters was Williams suffering a rib injury that required two medical timeouts, including a lengthy one after she dropped the first set in barely more than a half-hour.[195]

Williams picked up her play upon her return and gained a break in the eighth game of the second set. She closed out the set with an ace to force a winner-take-all scenario. Williams, though, turned the third set into a rout as she made only three unforced errors and rolled past Davenport 6-0 for her seventh Grand Slam title and first since claiming Wimbledon in 2003.[196]

"The last (slam) I won was I think Wimbledon, and that was exciting and fun," Williams said. "I love winning Wimbledon. I don't know. I feel that I needed to win the French because I've won two of each already except for the French. I've only one won. So I feel that, 'OK, I need to win another French Open so I can even them out.'"[197]

A spate of injuries forced Williams to withdraw during events in Paris, Dubai, and Amelia Island around a quarterfinal loss to her sister in Miami. She wasn't able to claim a second French Open title as she hoped because of the ankle injury suffered against Silvia Farina Elia in Amelia Island.[198]

Her struggles continued at Wimbledon, where she made a third-round exit, her earliest ouster at the all-England Club since her maiden appearance in 1998, with a straight-set loss to unseeded American Jill Craybas. Williams attributed some of the loss to the 85th-ranked Crybas to rust, which was reasonable considering she had played only 11 matches since winning the Australian Open.[199]

But the more shocking aspect of the loss was that her fearsome serve completely deserted her as Craybas broke Williams the first five times she served.[200]

"I shouldn't have lost this match," Williams said as she fought back the tears. "I hate to waste time, and I worked pretty hard the last week or so. But I guess you got to work more than a week, you know.[201]

Williams' woes continued, as did her slide down the WTA Tour rankings. A round of 16 loss in Toronto left her as the eighth seed heading into the U.S. Open. After three easy victories, a familiar opponent was waiting in an unfamiliar spot as her older sister and 10th-seeded Venus was her round of 16 opponent.[202]

It would be the earliest the sisters had met in a Grand Slam event since their first match in the 1998 Australian Open. Venus admitted that both of them did not want to talk about the possibility of meeting before the first week of the tournament was over, calling it "super strange." Serena again was trying to fight her way through injuries, having played just four matches before the 14th showdown between the siblings.[203]

Concerning form, the match looked more like the 1998 meeting than one between players who had combined for 11 Grand Slam titles. Venus took control in the later stages of the first set by staving off a set point while serving at 6-5 and forcing a tiebreak she eventually won. The second set may have been one of the easiest of Venus' career against her younger sibling as she won 7-6 (7-5), 6-2 to even the all-time series at seven wins apiece.[204]

Serena Williams' 2005 season started brightly, but ended with a whimper in Beijing where she tried to defend her title from the inaugural event last year. Wild-card entrant and 127th-ranked Tiantian Sun of China stunned Williams in straight sets. It was the worst loss for Williams since her professional debut against Miller as a 14-year-old, and the lethargy of such an underachieving season came home to roost in a listless performance that provided a shock scoreline.[205]

"I was very disappointed; I struggled all night, I played terribly," Williams admitted. "I never expected a tough match like this."[206]

The depression that Williams recounted in her book had at the very least, partially taken hold and left the talented 24-year-old somewhat directionless. Would things get better? Would they get worse? What would it take for Williams to simply find a spark to enjoy life again, let alone playing tennis at the pinnacle of her powers? Those answers were still many months away.

2006

Based on how she was feeling, one almost sensed Williams returned to Melbourne out of obligation as the Australian Open's defending champion. She was pushed to three sets in the first round against Li Na but showed champion's form in rolling past France's Camille Pin.[207]

The third round was where the rubber would begin to meet the road concerning quality opponents, and the 17th-seeded Hantuchova fit that description. The Slovakian who had failed to take a set off Williams in three previous matches looked like a world-beater in taking the opening set in 31 minutes by a 6-1 count. While she played better in the second set, there was a visible lack of passion by Williams as she eventually forced a tiebreak.[208]

But unlike previous title-winning years in 2003 and 2005, there would be no remarkable comeback. The lanky 23-year-old Slovakian found just enough points to outlast Williams in the tiebreak for her biggest win on the WTA Tour and further extended Williams' slide down the rankings, which was now going to carry her outside the top 40.[209]

"I just didn't play my best at all today," she said. "I was hitting balls every which direction. I didn't feel any of them."[210]

Taken in its proper context at that moment in time, this is a quote that says both everything and nothing. Williams accurately describes why she lost this match without revealing her mental and emotional processes. Now look at this quote again and combine it with how she described how she felt in her autobiography on the line while playing in that tournament (italics for emphasis):

"All I could think at that was that I *so* didn't want to be there, just at that moment. On the court. In Melbourne. Fighting for points I didn't care about in a match I really didn't care about. So what did I do? I cried. Right there on court … it started during one of the changeovers, but it continued when I went back out there to play, and it was such a low, despairing, *desperate* moment for me. I don't know how I managed to keep playing, but I kept playing because that's just what I did."[211]

Williams withdrew from events in Tokyo and Dubai, citing a lack of match fitness, as well as the Nasdaq 100, an event that she had won three times.[212] Her inability to defend rankings points at these events accelerated her downward slide in the rankings, sinking her below the top 100. By the time she resurfaced to play the Cincinnati Masters in July, she had entered the tournament ranked 139th in the world.[213]

Before the start of that tournament, Williams admitted she needed the time off mentally as well as physically to regroup from all that had happened over the previous two-plus years.

"I honestly just needed a mental break," she said ahead of her first-round match against the second-seeded Myskina. "I was going through a lot of stuff in my life, besides surgery and including surgery. It was a lot – a lot that not everyone will understand or ever know."[214]

Her on-court rehab included a stint in Florida with famed coach Nick Bollettieri, who appeared to have gotten some work in on Williams between her ears as well as between the lines. She noted that "he did a lot for me and my game."[215] But there was also a calmness that was evident as she embarked on a second climb to reach the No. 1 spot in the world.

"I hope to get a lot of satisfaction out of my game. I hope to go out and blow the joint up," Williams said. "My goals – I've never said them out loud. I just expect to do my best, and I think I play tennis best."[216]

Her return was a successful one as she conceded just four games to Myskina in a straight-set victory. Williams progressed to the semifinals before losing to Vera Zvonareva, but those all-important first steps had been taken.[217]

Williams would make only two more tournament appearances in 2006, losing in the semifinals in her hometown tournament in Los Angeles and in the round of 16 to Mauresmo at the U.S. Open in three sets.[218] While Williams refused to cite a lack of match fitness as a reason for the loss, a 35-shot rally in the third set with Mauresmo leading 3-2 that ended with her netting a backhand provided motivation for the Frenchwoman to win a break of service and eventually just her second win in 11 matches versus Williams.[219]

Despite what amounted to a lost year, Williams had done enough to climb back inside the top 100 in the rankings to No. 95.

2007

Inspiration comes in many places and takes many forms in everyone's life. After the U.S. Open, Williams had three months of down time away from competitive tennis. While continuing to progress back towards match fitness was a priority, her newfound sense of self also had to continue to improve. So in November of 2006, Williams, along with two of her sisters and her mother, Oracene Price, traveled to Senegal and Ghana as part of a tour arranged by UNICEF.[220]

It was the first time Williams had visited Africa, and while she conducted tennis clinics, she also did the daily work of the everyday volunteer health workers and also helped out in the immunization clinics. She met with the mothers of small children in Ghana as part of a concentrated effort to improve immunization awareness throughout the region of Nungua-Zongo.

"I'm definitely going back to the United States and talking to everyone about this experience," Williams said in a statement through UNICEF. "That way people can be more aware of diseases like malaria, and getting the polio vaccine, and all these vaccinations that are so necessary and so vital for children's health."[221]

During the Senegal portion of her trip, she was given a plot of land by the country's president Abdoulaye Wade. Williams expressed hope that she would be able to finance the construction of a school on those grounds.[222]

It appeared that the time off had done Williams well, but there were, rightfully, plenty of questions about her game by the time she arrived in Melbourne for the Australian Open. She was unimpressive in reaching the quarterfinals of a tune-up tournament in Hobart, and it was evident that Williams looked to be above her ideal playing weight heading into the first Grand Slam of 2007.[223]

Her mother, who had now become her full-time coach, admitted that she had her doubts as her daughter tried to figure out this next part of her life.

"What she did before the season, I couldn't tell you because I wasn't in Florida," Oracene Price said. "But when I look at her, I don't know.

I have my doubts. The level is there because even when she's not in the best of shape, she really gives people a hard time. So she has to get in the best of shape."[224]

Williams, who was ranked 81st in the world at the start of the Australian Open, was unseeded in the 128-field draw, and her first opponent was 27th-seeded Mara Santangelo of Italy. There were flashes of the Williams of old as she routed Santangelo 6-2, 6-1, needing barely more than an hour to advance. She made quick work of Anne Kremer in the second round and faced No. 5 seed Nadia Petrova in round three.[225]

Petrova had beaten Williams just once in the previous six meetings between the two, but the Russian was boldly confident heading into the match and claimed that no one feared either Williams sister.[226] Petrova carried that confidence well, winning the first set and took a 5-3 lead in the second. Williams, though, dug deep to hold serve and then break Petrova as she served for the match en route to forcing a decisive third set.

Williams broke Petrova twice in the third set, once at 3-1 and again at 4-2, and punctuated her victory with an ace on match point to reach the fourth round.[227]

The road would get no easier as Petrova would be the first of five seeded players in Williams' path to another Australian Open title. She cruised passes No. 11 seed Jelena Jankovic in the round of 16 before needing another escape act in the quarterfinals versus 16th-seeded

Shahar Peer of Israel.[228] Williams dropped the first set and was two points from defeat in the second before rallying. She went ahead 4-1 in the third set, but this time it was Peer who responded by winning five of the next six games and had a chance to serve out the match at 6-5.

Williams, though, broke Peer and won the next two games to close out the 2-hour and 34-minute match, denying Peer a historic milestone in her bid to be the first Israeli to reach a Grand Slam semifinal.[229]

In the semifinal against No. 10 Nicole Vaidisova, Williams started slowly before advancing in straight sets, and she earned a spot in the finals against the top-seeded Sharapova, who was now No. 2 in the world rankings and had all the momentum on her side. The Russian had won the U.S. Open the previous year and had gone 25-1 since that victory.[230]

Sharapova entered this final as much of a favorite as Williams did at Wimbledon in 2004, and win or lose, she would regain the world's No. 1 ranking on the WTA Tour following the match. But Williams showed her that she most certainly had plans for taking it back for herself as well.

Williams gave the Russian no quarter under the closed roof at Rod Laver Arena, and it looked as if the injuries and issues that had plagued Williams since completing the "Serena Slam" in 2003 had never happened. Here was Williams blistering first serves, searing forehands, and pouncing all over Sharapova's serve.

It was a complete reversal of fortune from the all-England Club less than three years before. By the end, Williams had won 6-1, 6-2 and left Sharapova in tears as she claimed her eighth Grand Slam title. But more importantly, there was genuine joy in Williams' smile as she bounced around the court before celebrating with her mother and coach.[231]

What followed was a poignant tribute to her half-sister Yetunde Price, to whom she dedicated the win, and the satisfaction of a staggering run through the field that made her the first unseeded player to win the Australian Open since Chris O'Neil in 1978.[232]

"I think I get the greatest satisfaction just of holding up the Grand Slam trophy and proving everyone wrong; I just love that," said Williams, who vaulted to No. 14 in the rankings with the title. "I just had so much fun out there today. I just made some great shots. It was just fun."[233]

The good times continued in Miami, where she ran her winning streak to 13 matches after rallying past Henin-Hardenne to win the Nasdaq 100. During that two-tournament run, she had defeated 11 seeded players.[234] Williams was forced to exit in the second round of the Family Cup Circle tournament due to a groin injury[235], and she finally regressed a little ahead of the French Open with a quarterfinal loss to Patty Schnyder in Rome.[236]

By the time Williams arrived at Roland Garros, she was a mystery. Would she show the form of an eight-time Grand Slam champion, or was she still working her way back into match shape? The slower pace of the clay, which requires patience and pounding from the baseline, would provide Williams a relatively accurate measuring stick of how far along she had come since the start of the year.

Williams was seeded eighth, and after an early blip in the first round had cruised into the quarterfinals opposite top-seeded Henin-Hardenne. Though the animosity from their match four years ago had dissipated, the desire to beat the Belgian remained. But on this day, Henin-Hardenne was the better player as Williams struggled all match. The result was a 6-4, 6-3 defeat that took less than 80 minutes and in a performance that she called "hideous and horrendous."[237]

The scenario would play out again at Wimbledon, where the seventh-seeded Williams again failed to solve the Belgian in the quarterfinals. Williams did make a better showing this time, extending the match to three sets despite calf and thumb injuries, but Henin-Hardenne improved her game in the decisive set to advance 6-4, 4-6, 6-3.[238]

For whatever reason, though the main one being she was the WTA's top-ranked player in the world, Henin-Hardenne had Williams' number at the last three majors of 2007. Williams did not drop a set in four matches as she carried her No. 8 seed into the quarterfinals against the Belgian. And once more, she came out on the short end of the scoreline, losing 7-6 (7-3), 6-1.[239]

It was a defeat that served as a junction for Williams' comeback. Yes, she had done many good things in getting to this point, but there was still plenty of work that had to be done to get better. Her surliness in the post-match interview underscored an understanding of that situation.

"I think she made a lot of lucky shots and I made a lot of errors," Williams said tersely while also ruling out lack of match fitness as a reason for her struggles against Henin.[240]

While Williams did not win another tournament the rest of the year, she climbed high enough in the WTA Tour rankings to seventh to make an appearance in the season-ending Tour Championships. However, that was a brief one-set cameo as a knee injury forced her to retire against Anna Chakvetadze.[241]

2008

The knee injury continued to be a hindrance to Williams, who was forced to skip the Australian Open tune-up events in Sydney, but she teamed with Mardy Fish to help the U.S. win the Hopman Cup in Perth, winning the mixed doubles match against Jelena Jankovic and Novak Djokovic for the deciding point.[242]

Williams' struggles in Grand Slam events continued, though the defense of her Australian Open title did not end in a defeat to Henin-Hardenne. It was again in the quarterfinals, but this time to Jankovic, who had skipped the singles match against Williams in the Hopman

Cup due to a leg injury. The third-seeded Serbian broke Williams seven times in her 6-4, 6-3 win, avenging a fourth-round loss to her the year before and briefly held the status of having a lifetime winning record against Williams.[243]

Instead of immediately returning stateside, Williams made her first professional appearance in India at the Bangalore Open. Both she and her sister were in the 32-strong field with Venus claiming the second seed and Serena the third. The two would meet in the semifinals, their first showdown in a tournament since their disinteresting fourth-round match in the 2005 U.S. Open.

In India, however, the sisters put up a Grand Slam-level effort as Serena advanced with a three-set win that also put her back on top in the sibling rivalry, 8-7.[244] The younger Williams finished off the successful trip by defeating Schnyder and climbed back into the top 10 in the WTA Tour rankings.[245]

That kicked off a 17-match winning streak that included titles in Miami and Charleston, highlighted by routing Henin-Hardenne 6-2, 6-0 in the quarterfinals in South Beach. Her three-set victory over Jankovic in the final gave her five titles in Miami, matching Graf for the most all-time.[246]

Her win streak came to an end in a three-set quarterfinal loss to Safina in Berlin, and she was forced to withdraw in the quarterfinals in Rome a week later against Alize Cornet due to a back injury.[247]

Williams was the fifth seed at the French Open, but No. 27 seed Katarina Srebotnik pulled off a third-round upset with a straight-set win. It was Williams' earliest exit from Roland Garros since 1999. Williams had fought off four set points in the opening set, but her inconsistent play afforded Srebotnik a fifth, which she converted when Williams missed a volley wide.[248]

The second set was more of the same with Williams squandering five break points and Srebotnik needing three match points and help from unforced errors by the American to finish off the match. While she acknowledged the Slovakian played well, Williams also noted that she "didn't play well in this tournament."[249]

The typical summer plan of Paris and England played out as Williams was seeded sixth for Wimbledon. And she played some of her best tennis of the year at the all-England club, not dropping a set in reaching the final, ending the surprising run of 133rd-ranked Zheng Jie in the semis around a pair of rain delays.[250]

For the first time in five years, the Williams sisters would be meeting in a Grand Slam final as Venus advanced from the opposite half of the draw. Despite being the seventh seed, the elder Williams did not face a seeded player until defeating No. 5 Dementieva in the semifinals.

The fortnight had marked the return of the sisters to the biggest stage of women's tennis, and they engaged in a thriller befitting their status in the final despite blustery conditions. Venus overcame a break in the first set to win 7-5, and she had a clear strategy on her service game, to force the ball into Serena's body.[251]

The younger Williams didn't lack for opportunities to gain on Venus' serve, but she converted only two of 13 break points. And befitting a four-time champion's savvy, the elder Williams wisely picked her spots to charge the net for serve-and-volley, winning points on all but three of her 18 approaches.[252] The result was a straight-set victory for Venus Williams that was also her fifth Wimbledon title.

The sibling rivalry was even once more, and while they would eventually take home the doubles title together, the loss left a sour taste in Serena's mouth in the competitive sense.

"I don't think I'm satisfied with the way I played. There's nothing for me to be satisfied about," she practically hissed.[253]

Unlike 2000 when Williams was not one of the top two ranked Americans to qualify for the Olympics, she had done so for the Beijing Games. But the quest for a singles gold medal ended in the quarterfinals against Dementieva, leaving her to settle for a second gold in doubles with Venus.[254]

The younger Williams was seeded fourth for the U.S. Open, and the competitive fire that burned from her loss at Wimbledon was evident in Flushing Meadow. She did not drop a set en route to her ninth Grand Slam title, but she needed to rally in both tiebreaks against Venus in a tense quarterfinal encounter. The tell that Serena had come all the way back came, ironically enough, in a point she lost during the second-set tiebreak.

Leading 4-2 and on serve, the sisters engaged in a 16-shot rally that Venus should have killed off at least three times before finally hitting an overhand smash into an empty court. Serena, though, scrambled back and forth well behind the baseline to get each sure-fire winner to extend the rally. This, ladies and gentlemen, was your No. 1 ranked player in the world ready to assume the mantle once more.[255]

Serena Williams regained the upper hand in the sibling rivalry, and after rolling past Jankovic in the final for her third U.S. Open title, she had the top spot in the WTA Tour rankings for the first time since 2003. The 6-4, 7-5 victory hid the fact Jankovic pushed Williams for more than two hours, but for Williams, it marked an internal moment where she realized there was so much more ahead of her in the sport.

"I feel like I have a new career, like I feel so young and I feel so energized to play every week and to play every tournament," she said. "I feel like there's just so much I can do in my career yet, and I've never felt like I've played my best tennis."[256]

Though Venus would again square the all-time series with a three-set win at the season-ending Tour Championship, it would be Serena who was named the Tour's Player of the Year as she ended the year ranked third in the world.[257]

2009

Fully refreshed, healthy, and motivated, Williams began 2009 at a tune-up event in Sydney ahead of the Australian Open. She showed some rust in needing to save seven match points over the course of her three wins before being routed by Dementieva in the semifinals,[22] but she arrived in Melbourne as the No. 2 seed.[258]

Much like New York the previous fall, Williams was dominant. She had some good fortune against Victoria Azarenka in the round of 16 as the Belorussian was forced to retire in the second set due to illness while leading 6-3, 2-4, and then rallied to defeat Kuznetsova in the quarterfinals.[259]

She avenged her loss to Dementieva in the semis, and her chance to win a 10th Grand Slam title would come against Safina, the younger sister of star tennis player Marat Safin. Perhaps Safin's elder brother would have put up more of a fight as Williams rolled to a 6-0, 6-3 win in just 59 minutes.[260]

It was a case of the stage being a bit too big for Safina, who was playing in her first Grand Slam final as well as having a chance to be the WTA's top-ranked player. Williams finished with 23 winners and stormed through the first set in 22 minutes, winning 18 of the last 20 points.[261]

Williams would lose in the semifinals in Paris and Dubai before her older sister denied her a record sixth title in Miami while taking a 10-

9 lead in the all-time rivalry. Then came a sudden dip in form in the clay-court season as she lost three straight matches without a victory in Marbella, Rome, and Madrid. Against 64th-ranked Francesca Schiavone in Madrid, Williams had to retire after the first set due to a knee injury.

Before the tournament, an ailing Williams had criticized the WTA Tour for its policy of fining players who pulled out of tournaments, even with injuries. She felt that the $75,000 fine for doing so was a bit drastic, noting, "I'm remodeling a house. I don't know about anyone else, but $75,000 is a lot of money to me. That's like my whole furniture bill … in this economy I'm not going to be writing out $75,000 checks."[262]

The two weeks off between the loss and the start of the French Open did Williams some good. She entered Roland Garros as the No. 2 seed but absorbed a tough three-set loss to Kuznetsova in the quarterfinals that lasted 2 hours and 46 minutes.[263]

By the middle of 2009, it had become clear the No. 1 spot was going to be contested among Williams, Dementieva, and Safina, who had reached the French Open final to show her run in Melbourne was no fluke. But Wimbledon was the Williams' domain, and the sisters again reminded everyone of it.

Serena, seeded second, did not drop a set in her first five matches, and No. 3 seed Venus did not lose a set all the way through to the final. While Safina had become an interesting story, the elder Williams put the young Russian and world No. 1 in her place with a 6-1, 6-0 thrashing in the semifinal in which she won the first two games in four minutes.[264]

Before that master class demolition, Serena needed three pulsating sets to put away Dementieva. The Russian had become one of the best returners in the game, blunting Williams' trademark powerful serves throughout the match. Williams fought off a match point in the decisive set down 5-4 and eventually broke the Russian to go ahead 7-6 before closing out the match on serve.[265]

So, once more, it was Venus vs. Serena at Wimbledon with more on the line historically for the elder Williams as she sought a sixth title at the all-England club that would tie her with King. She also carried a 20-match winning streak at Wimbledon into the match, including 17 straight-set victories in that span.[266]

But in the end, it was too much Serena. The younger Williams had a peerless service game in this final, never losing her serve against one of the all-time greats on this surface. Serena took control of the match in the second set, going ahead 4-2 when Venus double-faulted on break point and closed out her sister with another break on the fourth match point. Her 11th Grand Slam title moved her one behind King for sixth on the all-time list, and once more, she took the lead in the sisterly rivalry, which now stood 11-10 to Serena.[267]

Williams failed to reach the final in hardcourt events in Stanford, Cincinnati, and Toronto ahead of the U.S. Open,[268] and was the No. 2

seed in name only as Safina had remained the world's No. 1 player based on the sheer volume of points she picked up without losing any over various tournaments during 2009.

Williams' dominance was evident in Flushing Meadow as she ripped through her first five matches without dropping a set, but an old rival had made a new name for herself in New York that fortnight as Clijsters returned after an absence of more than two years following her 2006 retirement.

The Belgian accepted a wild-card into the Grand Slam event and stunned Venus Williams in three sets in the fourth round. After defeating 18th-seeded Li Na in the quarterfinals, Clijsters faced Serena for the first time since the 2003 Miami Masters semifinals.[269]

Despite her 30-month sabbatical, during which she had given birth to the family's first child, and playing just her third tournament in her comeback, Clijsters gave Williams everything she could handle in winning the first set. Williams was so frustrated with her play that she slammed her racket twice against the ground, which earned her a warning for racket abuse.[270]

That warning would loom incredibly large later in the match. The two could not find any separation in the second match, which Clijsters led 6-5 with Williams on serve as she tried to force a tiebreak. Down 15-30, Williams was called for a foot fault on her second serve by a lineswoman, which resulted in a double fault.

Though replays could show no obvious infraction, it was now 15-40, and Clijsters had two match points. Williams was irate at the call, arguing with the lineswoman before stomping back to the baseline to continue play. But for whatever reason, Williams did not let the issue rest. She approached the lineswoman a second time, ranting at her and at one point shaking her racket at her while she yelled.[271]

By this point, chair umpire Louise Engzell asked the lineswoman to approach and explain what had happened. Engzell then assessed Williams a point penalty for unsportsmanlike conduct, which turned out to be match point, which then gave Clijsters a victory.[272] At one point, the audio from the CBS feed picked up Williams in an incredulous tone saying, "I didn't say I would kill you! Are you serious?!" as referee Brian Earley tried to make sense of the situation.[273]

After about another minute of deliberation, the point penalty was confirmed and Williams threw her racket by her bag in disgust before going to shake hands with Clijsters.[274]

According to courtside reporters, they heard Williams use an expletive towards the lineswoman, with The Miami Herald adding that Williams told her she was lucky Williams was not "shoving this ball down your throat."[275]

The next day, Williams showed little if any remorse for her actions and refused to give an apology. What appeared to incense her more than anything was the spate of foot-faults that had been called against her after the violation had barely been called all year before the U.S. Open.

"I haven't been called for a foot fault all year until I got to New York, so maybe when I come to this tournament, I have to step two feet back," she fumed.[276]

The rest of the year would have no such controversies, with Williams winning the season-ending Tour Championship to reclaim the world's No. 1 ranking. She also beat older sister Venus twice in that event, once in group play and again in the final as she played a career-high 16 tournaments in 2009.[277]

2010

Williams began 2010 like a carbon copy of 2009. She lost to Dementieva in Sydney, though this time in the final, and defended her Australian Open title for her 12th career Grand Slam title. Williams dropped only one set en route to the final, to Azarenka in the quarterfinals, but did need a pair of tiebreakers to get past Li in the semis.[278]

In the final would be another Belgian making a surprising comeback, but this time it was Henin-Hardenne. Unlike most opponents who were content to take their chances and try to outslug Williams from the baseline in hopes she would make a mistake, the Belgian opted for the unorthodox approach of charging the net on the fast hardcourt surface.

Williams had taken the first set before Henin-Hardenne found her groove, reeling off 15 straight points to go from 2-2 in the second set to up 1-0 in the third. Williams fought off two break points to avoid an 0-2 hole in the deciding set and broke Henin-Hardenne twice to take a 5-2 lead before moving into a tie with Billie Jean King with her dozen Grand Slam titles.[279]

"I'm tied with you now, Billie. That was my goal," Williams said in her post-match address to the crowd.[280]

A leg injury would sideline Williams until the Rome Masters, where she lost in the semifinals to Jankovic. A trip to Madrid also turned up empty, but she arrived at the French Open as the top seed and had little trouble reaching the quarterfinals.[281]

There, though, she encountered all sorts of difficulties against Australian Samantha Stosur. Using a high kick serve to keep Williams off-balance, she quickly won the first set and looked on the verge of ousting Williams in the second with a chance to serve out the match. But a double fault at break point down 5-3 gave Williams a second lease on the match, and she took full advantage, winning a tiebreak to force a third set.[282]

Stosur, though, was able to regain her composure and even fought off a match point down 5-4 before uncorking two once in a lifetime shots to forge a break and take a 7-6 lead before winning the match.[283]

Willams, though, would get another chance at Grand Slam title No. 13 with her defense at Wimbledon. And she would get it with varying levels of ease as she did not drop a set in the fortnight at the all-England Club.[284] The defining moment of the tournament came against Sharapova in the fourth round when Williams fought off a set point and won the tiebreak 11-9 with a thunderous 125 mile-per-hour serve down the middle.[285]

Her victory over No. 21 seed Zvonareva in the final was a master class in a veteran's precision against an overwhelmed opponent. It took just 67 minutes as Williams fired nine aces and put all but two of her 33 first serves in play. And just like that, she moved ahead of King and into fifth on the all-time Grand Slams list.[286]

"It's kind of cool I was able to pass Billie," she said.[287]

Unfortunately for Williams, that would be where her year was unexpectedly derailed. While celebrating her victory the following week at a restaurant in Munich, Williams cut her right foot when she inadvertently walked on a broken glass while wearing sandals.[288]

The cuts required a total of 18 stitches, but there was far worse damage beyond the superficial wounds. By walking on it more, the glass cut tendons in her foot, causing the big toe on her right foot to droop. This required surgery upon her return to the U.S. that eventually wound up costing her the rest of 2010.

"My big toe was drooping, and I thought, 'My toe shouldn't be hanging like this,'" she recounted in September in her first public remarks after suffering the injury. "I saw a specialist in New York and had an MRI, and he said that I had a tendon that was torn."[289]

2011

But the after effects of that injury reached further than anyone could ever have envisioned. In February 2011, Williams was hospitalized due to a pulmonary embolism, which is a blood clot that enters the lungs, and then in March, she needed emergency treatment for a hematoma.[290]

Williams did not publicly disclose the treatment for the blood clot in her lungs, nor a second surgery on her foot in October 2010, until being hospitalized in March. She did release a statement saying that she was "praying and hoping this will all be behind me soon," while hoping to return to the WTA Tour in the summer.[291]

She remained faithful to her timeline and returned to tennis at Eastbourne in a tune-up tournament for Wimbledon. Williams lost so many ranking points that she dropped to 26th in the WTA rankings and had to accept a wild card to enter the 32-strong field. Her first match would be against Bulgaria's Tsvetana Pironkova, who would be no slouch considering she made the semifinals at Wimbledon in the other half of the draw while Williams was steamrolling to the title.[292]

The first set bore out the difficulty of facing Pironkova, who looked like a world-beater in thrashing Williams 6-1 in 27 minutes as the 13-time Grand Slam winner shook off nearly a year's worth of tennis inactivity and rust.[293] It would be Williams' mental toughness that was on display in this South Coast town of England where she would draw level by firing three successive aces to win the second set and eventually advance.[294]

"I was a little anxious, and I was missing a tremendous amount of shots," conceded Williams, who would lose to Zvonareva in the next round. "I was really focused just trying to get my feet to move, which was a task in itself."[295]

Recognizing her status as a four-time Wimbledon champion, the all-England club gave Williams the seventh seed for the 2011 tournament. She started slowly with a pair of three-set victories before easing past Maria Kirilenko in the third round, but there would be no third straight title as she lost to Marion Bartoli in the round of 16.[296]

The short-term pain of the early Wimbledon exit may have resulted in some long-term good as she won titles in Stanford and Toronto to kick off her hardcourt season.[297] Still, all those lost ranking points meant that she would have a challenging draw at the U.S. Open where she was seeded 28th.

Her first challenge in New York came in the third round against No. 4 seed Azarenka, but Williams won in straight sets.[298] That started a run of four victories against seeded players, which was highlighted by a semifinal win over current world No. 1, Caroline Wozniacki. It was a carefree ride to the final for Williams, who was appreciative of where she was from just six months ago when she was in a hospital bed.

"Six months ago I was in the hospital, and now I'm in the final," she said. "So I feel like, regardless of the result, I have been a champion for everyone out there who is fighting against all odds and staying positive."[299]

Williams would pair off with Samantha Stosur in the U.S. Open final, but for the second straight appearance in a three-year span, it would be an ugly confrontation with a match official that would grab the headlines instead of her on-court play.

Stosur had played a brilliant first set to take an early lead, winning the last 12 points, and Williams was struggling to do anything with her serve.[300] In the first game of the second set, Williams was serving 30-40, and during the point, let fly with a forehand that she thought was destined to be a winner. She screamed, "Come on!" as the ball traveled, and while Stosur was unable to return it, she did get her racket to it. According to the rulebook, this activated what is known as the "hinderance rule." This cost Williams the point, and therefore, the game to fall behind 1-0.

Chair umpire Eva Asderaki was slow to inform the crowd of what had happened, which resulted in a hail of boos as Stosur patiently waited them out to begin her service of the second game.[301] After winning the first point of that game, Williams admonished the umpire, drawing a code violation. Then, two games later during a changeover, Williams needlessly escalated the situation by engaging Asderaki again.

"If you ever see me walking down the hall, look the other way," she said. "You're out of control. You're a hater, and you're unattractive inside.

"Code violation for this? I expressed who I am. We're in America the last time I checked."[302]

The whole scene turned the crowd against Stosur, who was evidently rattled. Facing two break points down 2-1, Stosur fought her way back into the game and eventually held serve by giving Williams a dose of her own medicine with an ace clocked at 108 mph.[303] Williams would not threaten again and Stosur would celebrate her first Grand Slam title.[304]

For the second straight year, Williams was limited to six tournaments due to her variety of injuries, but she did finish with a 22-3 record and a No. 12 ranking.[305]

2012

Back in Australia for the first time since 2010, Williams opted for Brisbane as her warm-up to the Australian Open. That appearance was cut short after two wins due to an ankle injury she suffered in her second-round victory over Bojana Jovanovski.[306]

She was the 12th seed in Melbourne and looked like she was on her way to another potential Grand Slam title after three straight-set wins, but unseeded Ekaterina Makarova derailed those plans of a sixth Australian Open trophy in the fourth round. Williams' serve was unsteady at best and Makarova took full advantage in pulling off the upset.[307]

Williams won four Fed Cup matches in two rounds bracketing a loss in the quarterfinals in Miami and a clay-court title in Charleston. She picked up another win on her toughest surface in Madrid and reached the semifinals in Rome ahead of the French Open.[308]

There is something about the slower clay at Roland Garros that is a great equalizer for all underdogs, except perhaps when facing Rafael Nadal there. Typically, a big name is a first-round casualty at a Grand Slam event, and in her 47th such appearance, it was Serena Willams' turn to be the Goliath who fell.

Enter Virginie Razzano, a hometown French favorite who entered the match ranked 111th in the world. What everyone expected to be a first-round walkover for Williams turned into a three-hour clash of nerves, willpower, clutch shot-making, and at times, utter chaos. Williams ground to win the first set and was two points from victory in the second-set tiebreak, up 5-1, before Razzano shockingly won the next 13 points as she forced a decisive set.[309]

Williams seemed at a complete loss during this meltdown, which Razzano prolonged to put the 13-time Slam winner down in a 5-0 hole. Finally, the switch flipped. Williams started a furious rally to pull within 5-3. The partisan crowd, completely behind Razzano, roared with every point in the ninth game as Williams fought off the first match point.[310]

Then another, and another, and another. The two would trade haymakers from their respective baselines in a game that featured 12 deuces and 30 total points over 25 seemingly interminable minutes to the crowd. Eventually, Williams would astonishingly fight off eight match points in that game before Razzano watched a backhand by Williams sail long, resulting in her first, and to this day, her only first-round exit at a Grand Slam.[311]

"I tried, I kept going for my shots, which worked for me in the past, but it didn't work out today," said Williams, who finished with 47 unforced errors. "I just made too many errors today. That's not the way I've been playing. It's life."[312]

But as another empty sunset fell in Paris, another sunrise of hope would ascend at Wimbledon. There would be flashes of dominance, but Williams was also made to work as she was pushed to three sets by Jie Zheng in the third round and wildcard Yaroslava Shvedova in the fourth.[313]

In the finals against third-seeded Agnieszka Radwanska, Williams appeared to be cruising to her fifth Wimbledon title before an unchallenged opponent, Mother Nature, stepped in. The rain delay broke Williams' momentum as Radwanska leveled the match by taking advantage of Williams' inconsistencies with her forehand after the unexpected break.[314]

But Williams would regroup in the third set, breaking Radwanska twice to win her first Grand Slam title since her health scare and 14th overall.

"I can't even describe it. I almost didn't make it a few years ago," she said. "I was in the hospital, but now I'm here again, and it was so worth it. I'm so happy."[315]

Her fifth Wimbledon title was the start of a 21-match win streak that also saw Williams finally finish her elusive career "Golden Slam" with an Olympic gold medal at the very same all-England club she and her sister have dominated spanning three decades. Williams dropped just four games in the two medal matches, routing Azarenka in the semifinals before bulldozing Sharapova 6-0, 6-1 in the gold medal match.[316]

Everything Williams touched in that match turned to gold, firing ten aces and 24 winners as Sharapova yielded in just 63 minutes. It was her eighth straight win over Sharapova, and Williams doubled her pleasure with her sister as they swept through the women's doubles as well.[317]

Her winning streak ended in the quarterfinals in Cincinnati with a loss to Angelique Kerber, but it just meant that she had a chance to start a new one at the U.S. Open provided Williams could keep her temper in check. Six matches, six straight wins, highlighted by the rare double-bagel 6-0, 6-0 rout of Andrea Hlavackova in the fourth round, allowed Williams to sail into the final.[318]

Despite being the top seed and the No. 1 ranked player in the world, Azarenka was a decided underdog in the final given Williams' imperious form. And that played true to form in the first set as Williams needed barely more than a half-hour to move within one set of her 15th Grand Slam title.[319]

Williams, though, could not finish off Azarenka in that second set as she made 15 unforced errors while the Belorussian raised her game. The result was a third set that turned into a dogfight between two of the best on the WTA Tour. Azarenka forged ahead 5-3 in the decisive set, and Williams finally found that championship gear that so few of her peers have. She would win the last four games of the match, firing winners from all angles before Azarenka finally succumbed on match point with a long forehand.

The victory also pushed Williams past the $40 million mark in career winnings, an unprecedented amount for a female tennis player.[320]

Williams would cap her best professional year in style, claiming the season-ending Tour Championship for her seventh WTA title of 2012. She was named Player of the Year and finished No. 3 in the rankings behind Azarenka and Sharapova.[321]

2013

Considering all of her career accomplishments up to this point, it was hard to pinpoint any year as a "career year" for Williams given that she would win a major in a schedule that was limited to injuries, or in the case of her "Serena Slam," that it spanned two seasons. Her 2013 season, though, ranks as one of the best in WTA Tour history.

She pushed her winning streak to 16 matches with a title in Brisbane ahead of the Australian Open. But her hopes of adding a sixth title in Melbourne as well as a second such "Serena Slam" were thwarted in the quarterfinals by Sloane Stephens.[322]

In her first-round win, Williams twisted her ankle, and by the time she got to the second week of the tournament, her back had also been giving her issues. By the second set against Stephens, the pain got so intense that she smashed her racket into the court. The loss almost felt like a relief to Williams, who said that she was "thrown a lot of (curve) balls these two weeks."[323]

Williams would take nearly a month off before returning in Doha where she dropped a three-setter to Azarenka in the final. But a flare-up of the back injuries forced her to withdraw from the Dubai Open, which also marked the third time that she had committed to the event and failed to play.

"I feel terrible," she said. "I thought it would get better as the week went on, but it didn't. I don't want to keep pushing it and make it worse."[324]

The forced break sidelined her until late March when she finally captured her record-breaking sixth title in Miami at the Sony Open. She also maintained her mastery of Sharapova, rallying to defeat her in three sets in the final to extend her winning streak in the rivalry to 10 matches.[325]

Then the wins came fast and furious. A clay-court title in Charleston. Two wins in a Fed Cup tie versus Sweden. Another clay-court title in Madrid, then one in Rome.[326] By the time she arrived at Roland Garros, Williams sported a 23-match winning streak in all competitions during which she had dropped only two sets.[327]

There would be no first-round upset this time as she blasted American Anna Tatishvili 6-0, 6-1. Williams dropped just nine games in the next three matches before Kuznetsova slowed her briefly in the quarterfinals, extending Williams to three sets. The semifinal was a return to dominance as she flattened Sara Errani in just 46 minutes.[328]

That set up a final between Williams and the second-seeded Sharapova. Unlike the gold medal debacle, Sharapova came out aggressively and broke Williams early to grab a 2-0 lead. Williams responded by winning the next four games, but Sharapova proved stubborn and pulled even at 4-4. Williams, though, broke back and served out the first set.[329]

Though erratic at times, Williams still proved to have too much firepower for Sharapova. That was determined in the final game of the match in which Williams unloaded three aces, the last one clocked at 123 miles an hour on match point.[330] Eleven years later, Williams finally had her second French Open title, and she joined select company with Evert, Graf, and Navratilova as the only players in the Open Era to win every Grand Slam tournament twice.[331]

Williams had now won 74 of 77 matches since her shock defeat to Razzano at Roland Garros the previous year, and the rhetorical question she asked in the post-match address showed that she was still hungry for more.

"I definitely – I want to go out at my peak," she said. "That's my goal. But have I peaked yet?"[332]

Despite a stunning fourth-round loss to Sabine Lisicki at Wimbledon the following month, the answer to that question was a resounding "No." Williams won in her maiden appearance in Sweden and added another title in Toronto. Azarenka snapped Williams' 14-match win streak in the final of the Cincinnati Masters, which only seemed to further fuel Williams ahead of the U.S. Open.[333]

Williams was so dominant en route to the final at Flushing Meadow that she was not pushed to a tiebreak in her six victories. She recorded another double bagel, this time in the quarterfinals against 20th-seeded Carla Suarez Navarro.[334] Once more, Azarenka stood in the way in the final. And once more, the Belorussian gave her all she could handle for a while.

The match was played in blustery conditions which undoubtedly affected one side of the court. The result was a tight affair in which Williams grabbed the first set. She seemed on the verge of pulling away and led 4-1 before Azarenka finally righted herself and broke Williams twice when she served for the match, first at 5-4 and again at 6-5.[335]

The third set, though, was all Williams as she remained calm while the winds blew, rolling to her 17th Grand Slam title, which put her one behind Evert and Navratilova for third all-time. She also became the first female player to clear $9 million in winnings in a season and crossed the $50 million threshold for career winnings.[336]

"She's a champion, and she knows how to repeat that. She knows what it takes to get there," Azarenka said after just her second loss in 33 hardcourt matches that year. "I know that feeling, too. And when two people who want that feeling so bad meet, it's like a clash."[337]

Williams would close out the 2013 season on an 18-match winning streak, adding titles in Beijing and Turkey. She finished with nearly $12.4 million in prize money to go along with her 11 titles and was an easy selection for WTA Player of the Year.

2014

After such a spectacular year, it seemed unfair to ask for a duplicate effort of Williams, though she would give it her best effort. She successfully defended her title in Brisbane ahead of the Australian Open, where she was beaten in three sets in the fourth round by 14th-seeded Ana Ivanovic.[338] Once more, her back gave her issues over her last three matches in Melbourne, but Ivanovic also played well and recorded 33 winners. There was no shame in losing to her after setting an Australian Open record with her 61st singles victory.[339]

Williams won her next title in Miami, extending her tournament record there with her seventh triumph as she dropped just one set in the six victories. While there were no successful title defenses in Charleston and Madrid, there was one in Rome in her final tune-up for the French Open.[340]

But it all went sideways at Roland Garros, where she was blitzed in the second round by Spain's Garbine Muguruza. A promising player who entered the tournament ranked 35th in the world, the 20-year-old Muguruza handed Williams her worst Grand Slam defeat in a 6-2, 6-2 rout. It was an all-around ugly contest for Williams, who failed to win any points at the net and finished with just eight winners to 29 unforced errors while having her serve broken four times.[341]

"I don't think anything worked for me," she said. "You can't be on every day, and, gosh, I hate to be off during a Grand Slam. It happens."[342]

Wimbledon wouldn't be much better as Cornet rallied to spring a third-round upset that was marked by a rain delay of nearly five hours. The confidence from her victory over Williams in Dubai served as a springboard on a much bigger stage, one Williams and her sister had dominated for so many years between them.

"Everyone, in general, plays the match of their lives against me," said a frustrated Williams. "So I just have to always, every time I step on the court, be a hundred times better. If I'm not, then I'm in trouble."[343]

The hardcourt season provided a second wind as Williams won titles in Stanford and Cincinnati around a loss to her sister in the semifinals in Montreal.[344] Then it was time for the U.S. Open where she would seek a third straight title and an 18th Grand Slam that would match Evert and Navratilova as well as open up the question of where Williams stood among the all-time greats.

Once again, Williams stood as tall as the New York City skyline one can see in the distance from Flushing Meadow. Seven wins, zero sets dropped. No one could get more than three games off Williams in any of those 14 sets.[345]

Both Williams and Wozniacki struggled with their serve at the outset as there were five breaks in the first set. But Williams pumped out winners at a far more consistent rate, racking up 15 to the Dane's one in the first set. After breaking Wozniacki to open the second set, Williams was able to keep her serve on point and bookended the match with another break of her friend to wrap up her sixth U.S. Open title, matching Evert for the most in the Open era.[346]

"It was an unbelievable moment for me," Williams said. "Playing all those matches this summer really helped me to get my confidence up. I just needed that confidence and calmness. I've been practicing so hard and all that hard work was showing through today."[347]

Williams lost to Cornet for the third time in 2014, but she was forced to retire due to a virus in her match in Wuhan, China[348]. She lost to Stosur in the quarterfinals the following week in Beijing, but Williams capped off her Far East adventures with a title in the season-ending Tour Championships in Singapore. There, she bounced back from a round-robin loss to Simona Halep in her first match, beating the Romanian in the final.[349]

2015

Williams opted to bypass the warm-up events for the Australian Open and began her season in Melbourne proper. After two easy wins, she ran into some difficulty in the next two rounds and needed three sets to rally past both Elina Svitolina and Garbiñe Muguruza. Williams saved six break points to open the third set against the Spaniard, breaking her well in taking the decisive set 6-2.[350] Straight-set victories over Dominika Cibulkova and upstart American Madison Keys followed before another final-round date with Sharapova.[351]

It had now been more than a decade since the Russian last defeated Williams at the 2004 WTA Championships, and the losing streak had reached 15 matches in which Sharapova won a total of three sets.[352] While there was a clear lack of success, those scorelines obscured the fact that Sharapova could play well for stretches at a time and dictate play against Williams.

And such was the case in Melbourne. Williams tried to run away with the match early, winning 12 of the final 16 points to close out the first set after a brief delay to put up the roof at Rod Laver Arena.[353] Sharapova gamely withstood a barrage of aces in the second set and turned back a championship point down 5-4 by lacing a forehand and eventually forcing a tiebreaker.

Williams would squander a second match point as Sharapova closed within 6-4, but she uncorked her 18th ace of the match to finish off the Russian for her sixth Australian Open title. The 19th Grand Slam of her career left her behind only Graf's Open era record of 22 and third all-time as Williams slid ahead of Evert and Navratilova and into a tie with Helen Willis Moody.[354]

"Standing here with 19 championships is something I never thought would happen," Williams said while accepting her trophy. "I went on the court with a ball and a racket and a hope. It's inspiring for those of you out there who want to be something or for whatever you want to do when you grow up. You never know who you're going to inspire; so I'm so honored."[355]

Williams would follow up the triumph with a Fed Cup win in Argentina, but there was a bigger headline waiting. She would end the sisters' 14-year boycott and participate at the WTA event in Indian Wells for the first time since the controversies that swirled around them in 2001.

She made the announcement in an essay released by Time Magazine for its February 4 issue a full five weeks before the start of the tournament.[356] Williams recounted the details of her day in the 2001 finals in vivid detail, noting how "it has been difficult for me to forget spending hours crying in the Indian Wells locker room in 2001, driving back to Los Angeles feeling as if I had lost the biggest game ever…"[357]

The snide comments from Russian Tennis Federation president Shamil Tarpischev, who jokingly called Serena and Venus "brothers,"[358] and earned a one-year ban from the ITF for his comments also weighed on the younger Williams' mind as she reached her decision. In the end, Williams chose forgiveness, closing her essay with the following:

"I have faith that fans at Indian Wells have grown with the game and know me better than they did in 2001. Indian Wells was a pivotal moment of my story, and I am a part of the tournament's story as well. Together we have a chance to write a different ending."[359]

Everything about the playing part of the tournament went well for Williams as she dropped just one set in her four victories in reaching the semifinals. But a knee injury while practicing for her match against Halep scuttled those plans and Williams was forced to withdraw before the match, allowing Halep a walkover into the finals.

Williams said that she exhausted all of her options to avoid a different outcome in addressing the crowd for the reasoning, even resorting to an injection. She noted that "if this were any other event, I probably wouldn't have considered it. But I wanted to give 200 percent. It just wasn't meant to be this year."[360]

She would recover to play her favorite non-Grand Slam tournament, winning the Miami Open for an eighth straight time as Navarro avoided a second double bagel defeat to Williams by winning two games in the first set. Another pair of Fed Cup wins in Italy kicked off her clay-court season with empty results in Madrid and Rome.[361]

For the first time since 2003, Williams entered the French Open as the defending champion, and while she accomplished the feat, it can be argued that it was the most laborious of her 20 Grand Slams to that point in her career. She needed to rally past unheralded German Anna-Lena Friedsam in the second round and again in the third versus Azarenka.[362]

The task to overcome a first-set deficit was tougher still against Stephens in the round of 16 as Williams was three points from defeat down 5-4 and love-15 in the second set. She recovered to win the next four points and avoided the same fate as her sister, who lost to Stephens in the first round. The key point in the third set came when

Williams swatted away a break point with an ace and was not threatened thereafter.[363]

Williams would again need three sets in both the semifinals and her final versus Lucie Safarova. An illness forced her to skip practice the day before the final, and it showed at times throughout the last two sets. Williams squandered a two-break lead in the middle set, part of an erratic effort that included 11 double faults and 42 unforced errors.[364]

She fell behind a break in the third set before finally coming to life, winning the final six games as Williams became the first player to win the first two majors of the calendar year since Capriati in 2001.[365]

The mere idea of Williams contending for a calendar Grand Slam captivated sports media more than the fact that she had a chance to complete a second "Serena Slam" if she could win a sixth title at the all-England club. Wimbledon continued to be like a home away from home for Williams and she had little trouble in her first three matches.[366]

In the fourth round, though, elder sister Venus awaited. It was the first time the two were playing since 2009, and Venus was seeded 16th as injuries had taken their toll on the fellow five-time Wimbledon champion. And younger Serena would show little remorse, winning the first eight points of the match to dictate its tone.[367]

As always, Venus would fight in a calm and collected nature. After dropping the first set, she ground out to a 3-2 lead on serve in the second. But by this point, Serena was just too much to take on at her current level. Younger sis won the final four games of the match, and Serena finished with 22 winners to her older sister's six.[368]

"It's never easy to play someone you love and care about," Serena said after taking a 15-11 lead in the all-time rivalry. "You just play for the competition and enjoy the moment."[369]

Azarenka continued to be a persistent tough out with Williams needing three sets to bounce her in the quarterfinals. And Sharapova continued to be valiant yet overmatched as Williams dispatched her in the semis.[370] That left the 20th-seeded Muguruza standing between Williams, a 21st Grand Slam title, and breathless anticipation over the first potential calendar Grand Slam since Graf's "Golden Slam" of 1988.

The 21-year-old Spaniard showed few nerves in her Grand Slam final debut, taking a 4-2 lead before Williams asserted herself to win nine of the next ten games to move within one game of her sixth Wimbledon Venus Rosewater Dish.[371] Though the plucky Spaniard won the next three games to give the glimmer of hope for a third set, the wily and now 33-year-old Williams shut down any chance of that by breaking Muguruza at love to close out the match.[372]

"It would be really good to have this opportunity to go into New York being American with that amazing New York crowd," Williams said as the Grand Slam questions began in earnest. "Hopefully, people would be really cheering me on to like push me over the edge and give me that extra strength I need to go for this historic moment."[373]

Given her injury history, Williams was about to take no chances over the summer before the U.S. Open. She pulled out of a clay event in Sweden due to an elbow injury and played in two hard-court events ahead of that Grand Slam, reaching the semifinals in Toronto and winning in Cincinnati.[374] Now the moment had finally come, with the biggest player in tennis on the biggest stage in America and arguably the world: The U.S. Open with New York City as the backdrop to potential history.

The media day in which the tournament draw was announced was an event to itself. Williams and her coach Patrick Mouratoglou parried with reporters about her chances to complete the Grand Slam, where her legacy in the sport was at that moment, and how to deal with the intense pressure that would surely ratchet exponentially with each victory at Flushing Meadow.

"It's going to be very important to have perspective," Mouratoglou said. "She has to be conscious of everything she's achieved, all the records she has. This is not that important. I understand for the press it is, but for her, it shouldn't be.

"If you give it too much importance, it's like you play with a bag of 20 kilos on your back. That is not going to work."[375]

So here it was. Seven matches from immortality, in a sense. What was lost in the commotion of completing the calendar Grand Slam is that Williams would also equal Graf with her 22nd career Grand Slam title. It seemed like everything was aligning for Williams.

Her first-round match proved to be barely that. Vitalia Diatchenko was forced to retire after just eight games and 21 minutes, trailing 6-0 2-0, due to a foot injury she suffered in pre-match warmups.[376] Much was made about her decision to even play through the injury, but the Russian refused to pass up on the near $40,000 payday that goes to first-round U.S. Open losers.[377]

Next up was Dutch qualifier Kiki Bertens, who put up slightly more resistance as Williams cruised in straight sets. She faced her first bout of adversity against American compatriot Bethanie Mattek-Sands, who was ranked 101st entering the match. The underdog played a near-flawless first set, breaking Williams twice and making just two unforced errors.

Williams found her service game in the second set and eventually found separation by winning the final two games. The third set was little more than perfunctory as Williams swept Mattek-Sands aside in 25 minutes, overcoming her first scare of the fortnight and reaching the fourth round.[378]

The first seeded opponent in Williams' path was No. 19 Madison Keys, who had not dropped a set in reaching the round of 16. Williams' serve was untouchable, and she broke Keys to go up 5-3 to win the first set. While a game opponent, Keys eventually faltered into another break midway through the second set and that was more than enough daylight for Williams to advance to the quarterfinals against her sister and 23rd-seeded Venus.[379]

Cue the hype machine.

This would be the 14th Grand Slam meeting between the siblings and the 27th overall as professionals. The rivalry, once uneven as two awkward teenage girls tried to navigate their way around each other's feelings while playing, was now steeped with respect and pride as they talked about the other's game.

"For me, I'm playing the best player in the tournament, and that's never easy," Serena said. "She's beaten me so many times. I've taken a lot of losses off of her – more than anybody. She's a player that knows how to win, knows how to beat me, and knows my weaknesses better than anyone … she's the only player in the draw I don't want to play – not only because she's my sister, but because for me, she's the best player."[380]

"I don't think anyone wants to be a spoiler. I think people love to see history being made," the elder Williams said. "No one is out to be a spoiler, but at the same time, you're focused on winning your match even though the circumstances are really much different than you (would want)."[381]

The U.S. Open was already an expensive ticket, but the quarterfinal sibling showdown made it one of the toughest in an already tough city when the best of the best play. The day of the tournament, the average ticket price to get into Arthur Ashe Stadium to see the sisters play was near $1,000, more than double what it was shortly after the draw was announced.[382]

Serena started fast in this one and did not make an unforced error until the seventh game, and by the time that one was over, she had broken Venus twice for a 5-2 lead and easily won the first set.[383]

In the second set, the issues that plagued Serena's serve throughout the tournament came to the forefront as she double-faulted on break point to give Venus a 3-1 lead. This time it was the older sister with a pair of breaks as she forced the third set by rolling 6-1. But one of the things Serena had proven time and again by this point in her career is her steely resolve. And the first game of the third set proved to be such a time to show it.

Leading 30-15, Serena blistered an ace wide and roared in approval afterward. She followed it up with another ace to take the first game, sending a message that her serve was back on point and that Venus would need to dig a little deeper to stop her younger sister's bid for a calendar Grand Slam.[384]

Serena then goes up a break to lead 2-0 before Venus makes her last stand. She is a point away from breaking back to keep the match on serve, but Serena uncorks a 110 mile per hour ace down the middle to send it to deuce. There would not be a second break point opportunity for Venus as Serena cracks a service winner to make it 3-0.[385] The rest of the match remains on serve, and the younger Williams closes out in style with an ace clocked at 107 mph. It is onto the semifinals after a high-quality match against arguably the toughest opponent of Serena's career.[386]

The two sisters shared a warm hug at the net, something that meant more to Serena in the post-match interview than it did moving two wins away from history.

"It's the greatest story in tennis. Because of where we come from and how we started," she said. "It doesn't get better for us (now). And the people that we've inspired."[387]

Nearly everyone felt that Williams' semifinal opponent, Robert Vinci, would provide little resistance. Ranked 43rd in the world heading into the match, Vinci had failed to take a set off Williams in any of their previous four matches.[388] In fact, Vinci did not even defeat a seeded player en route to the semifinals, getting a walkover into the quarterfinals when 25th-seeded Eugenie Bouchard was forced to withdraw due to a concussion suffered when she slipped and fell in the locker room the day before that scheduled round of 16 match.[389]

Around that walkover, Vinci needed three sets in each of previous three matches to earn the spot opposite Williams. Everything about this match screamed rout for Williams, and the first set did as well as she won 6-2 in just over a half-hour.[390] But as Mouratoglou would later point out, Williams' footwork was off throughout the first set. And for Williams, that is the foundation that is everything; it sets up her punishing groundstrokes, it sets up her unreturnable serves, and it provides the calmness that leads to success. When it goes away, that is when any great player, even one with 21 Grand Slam major titles, is vulnerable. And so it was here, with a savvy veteran opponent in Vinci ready to capitalize.

She began to swing the match in the second set, breaking Williams to go up 3-2 and rode that break to force the winner-take-all third. Williams, though, appeared to have righted herself and broke Vinci to go up 2-0 after slamming a volley on break point. But it would be her service game betraying her once more, double-faulting on break point that allowed Vinci back into the match at 2-1.[391]

By this point, it was evident that Vinci was not going away and that Williams was going to have to beat her. After all, the Italian did not have the weight of the tennis world on her shoulders as a global audience watched in hopes of history being made. The two remained on serve until the seventh game where it finally unspooled for Williams.

She recovered from a pair of double faults to force deuce and then sizzled an ace at 126 miles per hour. But with Williams having a chance to serve for the game, it was Vinci who provided the breakthrough moment, capping a high-quality rally with a half-volley into the open court. She would finish the break to go up 4-3, and everything was up for grabs.[392]

Williams made one last push, earning two break points the next game, but she squandered them just as easily as she earned them with her 36th and 37th unforced errors of the match. Number 38, though, proved to be equally damaging as it gave Vinci the game, and the Italian could serve out the match for one of the biggest upsets in tennis history given the stakes of the match.[393]

Williams did not offer much about her emotions in the post-match interview, telling reports that, "I don't want to talk about how disappointing it is for me."[394] But Navratilova, an expert on such things given her dominance, noted that Williams "lost to the Grand Slam more than anything else."[395]

That loss would be the last match for Williams in 2015. She skipped the season-ending Tour Championship in Singapore, citing emotional and physical exhaustion as well as an elbow injury that had been bothering her late in the season.[396] But even at the age of 34, Williams showed just how dominant her game was in what's supposed to be a younger player's game; she and Sharapova were the only two players to make more than one Grand Slam semifinal in 2015.[397]

2016

With the talk of a calendar Grand Slam now in the past, the next milestone everyone turned their attention to was 22. That was the number of career Grand Slam titles Graf had won, the most in the Open era, and Williams would match her with the next one. But despite her dominance on the WTA Tour, that window of opportunity would close slightly with each major she did not win. And with only four per year, there are not that many chances to add to that total.

Williams kicked off her season at the Australian Open and stormed into her seventh Melbourne final without dropping a set. But her hopes of a seventh Aussie Open title were thwarted by Angelique Kerber, whose play after losing the first set belied her status as a first-time Grand Slam finalist as she rallied to stun Williams. Much the same way Vinci kept the ball in play at Flushing Meadow the previous fall, Kerber did the same, only with more pace to pressure Williams into unforced errors on her forehand.[398]

She did not play again until Indian Wells, where this time she was joined by Venus as her older sister ended her boycott of the California tournament. It was another finals appearance and another loss for Serena, as Azarenka won in straight sets.[399]

Her first win of the season did not come until Rome, where she beat Keys in the final for that clay-court title. Then it was back to Ronald Garros, where she again came one win shy of defending her French Open title. This time, Muguruza would deny Williams her historic milestone, winning in straight sets and establishing herself as perhaps the best of a new generation that might finally be ready to challenge Williams.[400]

It was not as much Williams losing this one as it was the Spaniard winning it, displaying the kind of power Williams had rarely faced throughout her storied career, save maybe for her sister. Muguruza even showed a little resolve herself, closing out Williams in the final game at love on serve after squandering away four match points the previous game.[401]

Despite losing back-to-back Grand Slam finals, there was never a sense of panic or worry from the Williams camp. Both she and Mouratoglou had been effusive in their praise of Kerber, and now Muguruza, in their maiden Grand Slam title victories. Now the issue was whether Williams had enough to hold off the next generation.

That question would be answered at one of her favorite stomping grounds, the SW 19, or as everyone else knows it, Wimbledon. Unless Williams lost, it only became news if she got pushed to three sets, and that only happened in the second round against Christina McHale.[402]

Williams would get a second chance against Kerber in the finals at the all-England Club. Unlike those previous finals where Williams' serve betrayed her, the fast grass at Wimbledon would become her ally. She rifled 13 aces, part of a blistering performance that saw her drop just five points on her first serve and face only one break point in winning 7-5, 6-3.[403] After winning her seventh Wimbledon title, she held two fingers aloft from each hand to her player box to mark the moment and could finally exhale after what seemed to be an interminable stretch of trying to match Graf.

"Trying so hard to get there, finally being able to match history, which is pretty awesome," Williams said. "My goal is to win always at least a slam a year. It was getting down to the pressure. I just needed to keep calm, be confident, just play the tennis that I've been playing for well over a decade."[404]

Williams was denied a second Olympics gold medal in women's singles in Rio de Janeiro as she lost to Svitolina in the round of 16. That was her lone tournament before the U.S. Open, where she again made a semifinal exit in a straight-set defeat to 10th-seeded Karolina Pliskova.[405] That loss, coupled with the loss of rankings points from playing just eight tournaments all year, also ended Williams' 186-week reign as the No. 1 player on the WTA Tour, a match she also shared with Graf.[406]

2017

The record will show Williams participated in two tournaments tournament in 2017, a warm-up event in New Zealand in which she had a sloppy second-round loss and the Australian Open. But in the "go big or go home" manner that has now been her calling card as she chases immortality with every Grand Slam, No. 23 will be remembered fondly for a multitude of reasons.

Once more, the early rounds were a parade of straight-set victories against overmatched opponents. Not that the seeded players gave her much trouble in Melbourne, either. No. 16 seed Barbora Strycova and ninth-seeded Johanna Konta also fell by the wayside in the next two rounds. In the semifinals, fellow 35-year-old Mirjana Lucic-Baroni made a spectacular run to get to that point, but Williams would show no mercy in a 6-2, 6-1 rout that took a mere 50 minutes.[407]

But even Serena's chase for historic Grand Slam No. 23 was upstaged to a great extent by her older sister. Seeded 13th, Venus Williams had her section of the bracket open up when No. 4 seed Simona Halep lost in the first round and then a little further when seventh-seeded Muguruza lost in the quarterfinals.

Williams then needed every bit of her poise and experience to outlast Coco Vandeweghe in the semifinals, staving off 12 of 13 break points in rallying for a three-set victory.[408] So the Australian Open final was going back to the future. It would be the first time the sisters were meeting in a final since 2009, and the first time it was happening in Melbourne since 2003. Both Williamses were eager to reunite on the grand stage, with Serena calling it "probably the moment of our career thus far," and Venus noting that "when I'm playing on the court with her, I think I'm playing the best competitor in the game."[409]

Now nineteen years after the two had met as professionals for the first time in a second-round match at the Australian Open as gangly teenagers, the Williams sisters looked at each other across the court with yet another Grand Slam title at stake. Either way, it would be the 30th such title won by either Serena or Venus with the younger sister looking to win in a Grand Slam final over the older one for the seventh time in nine tries.[410]

While the match lacked some of the quality the two had put forth in those battles of yesteryear, there was a definite edge to the final. The two traded breaks over the first four games, and it was Venus who was showing more on-court emotion than usual. Not that Serena lacked her trademark fire, she smashed a racket at the end of the third game following a lost point due to slipping.[411]

Serena would break Venus a third time, which was enough to carry her to the first set. By this point, her serve was proving problematic for her older sister as she reeled off 11 straight points, bridging the sets.[412] The match stayed on serve for the first six games of the second set before Serena unleashed a wicked backhand on her second break point of the game for a 4-3 lead.

The younger Williams would successfully serve out for the title, moving ahead of Graf with her 23rd Grand Slam title that also put her one behind Australian Margaret Court for the most of any player in tennis.[413] The ceremony for Serena's seventh Australian Open title was a poignant one as the sisters traded sobriquets of praise, but it was their half-sister Isha Price, who offered an interesting perspective on the sisters' perseverance for now almost two full decades worth of professional tennis.

"Long story short, I don't think people actually understand the significance of what they see, these two players, who literally for generations have been able to transcend what they do," said Price, who chose to watch the match from the hotel rather than the players' box. "And it's very difficult to watch, listen, hear commentary, all of that. We watch tennis on mute. It's hard.

"To keep your body in optimal shape to be able to perform at this level consistently over 20 years is an incredible feat. But you still have the conversation where it's not enough."[414]

Depending on one's perspective, what followed next borders on amazing considering that it quickly pushed the historic victory to the backburner. In mid-April, Williams put a photo on the social network Snapchat, something she had quietly been doing once a week over the previous five months. Only this time, she inadvertently made the picture public, and with the caption "20 weeks" in the picture, it did not take long for the world to realize she was pregnant.[415]

In one of those "it's funny when you look back at it" moments, Williams recounted the story during a TED talk in an interview with Gayle King:

"I was on vacation, taking time for myself, and I have this thing where I've been checking my status and taking a picture every week. I've been just saving it, but you know how social media is – you press the wrong button and. ... My phone doesn't ring that much, and 30 minutes later, I'd missed four calls. So I picked it up and realized, 'Oh no.'"[416]

The announcement came approximately four months after Williams, who found out she was pregnant near the start of the Australian Open, and fiancé Alexis Ohanian announced their engagement in late December 2016. But the timeline of the pregnancy revealed something amazing, that Williams won the Australian Open while she was pregnant

Mouratoglou said he did not know until "15 days ago," which would have put the date on April 6 based on when his interview in the New York Times ran.[417] But the French-born coach, widely credited with reviving Williams' career at an elite level since he came on board in 2012, thinks Williams will be more than ready to take aim at the last name above her for Grand Slam titles, Margaret Court, when she returns.

"What is fabulous is all these challenges, and now there's a new challenge that's incredible," said Mouratoglou, who has been with Williams for 10 of her 23 Slam victories. "She'll be over 35 and a new mother trying to win Grand Slams."[418]

While there is no telling the effects pregnancy will have on Williams, not playing tennis for the remainder of 2017 will probably do her joints some good. She has regularly been providing updates of her baby bump on her social media accounts, and ever the savvy businesswoman, some of those pictures have doubled as promotions for her signature line of clothing.[419]

The call to motherhood came at a time when Williams had just regained the WTA's No. 1 world ranking, something she will technically lose again in the coming weeks as she fails to defend her rankings points from previous tournaments. But when she does return in 2018, it is already clear that she is the queen of women's tennis until she is dethroned.

Chapter 6: Serena's Top Rivals

Given how many times Serena faced her older sister Venus in the finals of Grand Slam events that was documented throughout the prior chapter, there is little to add. The main thing to be remembered is that they raised the game of women's tennis concerning both public profile and quality to an unprecedented level.

It is admittedly difficult to call it a "rivalry" because there is no hatred. After a while, it does not make for "good copy" to lead into one of their matches. At first, the combination of genuine curiosity and skittish play when the sisters faced off against each other were contributing factors in their coverage. It was in many ways a novelty act since the only other sibling act on either tennis circuit is the Bryan brothers, who exclusively play doubles together.

Only after Venus' career took off, and Serena's shortly after that, did the public begin to embrace them. Once their father Richard started to let the sisters play on the court as well as the sisters making it a point to praise the other's play as part of the focus of the rivalry, that was when it took off in the public's imagination.

Perhaps the most impressive stretch of their rivalry was the span from 2001-03 when they met in the finals of six grand slams, including five in a row from 2002-03, over seven head-to-head meetings.[420] The "Serena Slam" came at the expense of her older sister, who did not get a set off her in any of those four finals.

Even the few wins Venus has gotten have come in grueling fashion. She has not defeated Serena in straight sets in any head-to-head match since winning the 2008 Wimbledon final.[421] That also serves as the last of Venus' seven Grand Slam titles, and since then, Serena has won 15 of her 23 Slams, including the 2009 Wimbledon and 2017 Australian Open finals over her older sister.

Since Serena's reign of success spans a generation, many of her primary rivals feature an "if only" feel to them because they lacked staying power. Take the case of Hingis, whom Williams holds a 7-6 all-time lead against.

Hingis' rise to power was shockingly quick. She turned professional in 1996, won a Grand Slam doubles title at 15 at Wimbledon and became the youngest Grand Slam title winner the following year at the Australian Open en route to becoming the world's No. 1 player. Hingis won three Grand Slam titles in 1997, missing out on a calendar Slam only by losing to Iva Majoli in the finals of the French Open.

By the time she lost to Serena Williams in the 1999 U.S. Open final, she had already won six Grand Slam singles titles, and there was every reason to believe that she would be at the forefront of women's tennis with the Williams sisters, Davenport, Pierce, and a rejuvenated Capriati. But the power game that the Williams brought into women's tennis was something Hingis never truly caught up with despite her excellent all-around game.

And injuries also took their toll. The two ankle surgeries around her appearance in the 2002 Australian Open final in which she squandered four match points and lost to Capriati hastened her decision to retire. While she did make a brief comeback in 2005 and 2006, it never rose to a level that would challenge Williams.

Williams and Hingis met in only one other final besides the 1999 U.S. Open, the 2000 Canadian Masters in which Serena retired in the third set due to a knee injury. Williams won the last three meetings between them, including a 2001 U.S. Open semifinal.[422]

Capriati was one of the original power players who was expected to revolutionize the game with Graf and Seles. Much was made of her early splash on the WTA Tour at the age of 14 and the dizzying heights that followed with an Olympic gold medal at 16 as well as her fall from grace following her arrests for shoplifting and marijuana possession.[423]

The rivalry that followed Capriati's return was well-played as Williams won 10 of the 17 matches. Capriati won four of the first five, including victories at both Roland Garros and Wimbledon as Williams was learning what it took to win Grand Slam titles.[424] Capriati, in fact, is one of the few players to get the better of Williams in the majors, winning four of their seven clashes in such events. They never met in a Grand Slam final, with six of the contests coming in the quarters, and the only semifinal appearance a three-setter won by Williams in the 2002 French Open semifinals.[425]

The last meeting, a victory by Capriati in the 2004 U.S. Open quarterfinals, included line calls against Williams that were so egregiously bad that USTA official Arlen Kantarian called the following day to apologize.[426] The match wound up being one of the accelerants for video review on serves and the institution of using robotic cameras such as HawkEye on both the WTA and ATP tours.

A tight rivalry that could have been a special one in the sense that it could have lasted for at least a continuous decade had she not opted to raise a family would have been against Henin. Williams holds a 10-8 lead in that all-time series, though it was broken up by the 2 ½ years Henin left the WTA Tour. The seven-time Grand Slam winner won three straight French Open titles and may have been the one player aside from her sister who gave Williams fits because Henin had arguably the greatest backhand in women's tennis in the 2000s.

The two split six Grand Slam matches across all four majors with Williams winning the only final they contested in those tournaments at the 2010 Australian Open. While Henin will always be remembered for the 2003 French Open and the subsequent revenge match Williams won at Wimbledon the following month, Henin also beat Williams in three majors in 2007 – the French Open, Wimbledon, and the U.S. Open.[427]

She became a foil to Williams' power game with the spin she would put on her backhand as well as constant changes in strategy to keep her off balance by "trying to put more pressure, heavy balls … try to play very deep and push her back."

"I was trying to change the rhythm, also, trying to come to net, slice a little bit, and that helped," she added. "Sometimes it worked, sometimes it wasn't enough because what is very tough with Serena is that mentally, she can play her best points in the important moments."[428]

While these are the players who got the best of Williams over the years, there are a few players whose persistence have gotten them plenty of chances to beat her over the years but with little success.

At the top of that list is Sharapova, whose losing streak to Williams now spans 12 years and 18 matches since winning the 2004 WTA Championships. Williams has ended seven of Sharapova's Grand Slam bids during that run, including twice at the Australian Open finals (2007, 2016) and the 2013 French Open final.[429]

But what added fuel to this one-sided rivalry was a 2013 Rolling Stone profile on Serena that included what was believed to be her ruthless critique of Sharapova's personal life while talking to Venus on the phone, with Serena saying, "She begins every interview with 'I'm so happy. I'm so lucky' – it's so boring. She's still not going to be invited to the cool parties. And hey, if she wants to be with the guy with a black heart, go for it."[430]

The author of the article implied the "guy" in question was Grigor Dimitrov, a player Serena Williams was rumored to have dated before Sharapova. The article moved in that gap in June between the French Open and Wimbledon, and it provided more than enough grist for almost every publication, and in particular every British tabloid newspaper, to put up breathless headlines before the tournament at the all-England Club.

Four days after the story appeared and two before Wimbledon, Sharapova lit into Williams for her comments and added plenty of fire to what was now a she-said, she-said "Mean Girls" fight being played out publicly.

"If she wants to talk about something personal, maybe she should talk about her relationship and her boyfriend that was married and is getting a divorce and has kids," the Russian shot back, making a reference to Mouratoglou.[431]

Sharapova further criticized Williams' comments in the article regarding a rape case involving the sexual assault of a 16-year-old girl in Steubenville, Ohio, and Williams quickly offered an apology to the girl's family for that. The following day, Williams said she apologized to Sharapova at the players' pre-tournament party, saying that she "made it a point to reach out to Maria because she was inadvertently brought into the situation by assumptions made by the reporter."[432]

While Williams' mastery over Azarenka is nearly as lopsided of the one she has over Sharapova, what makes the Belorussian stand out is the fact that she has played Williams 10 times in Grand Slam matches without getting a victory. That accounts for nearly half of their 21 matches, of which Williams has won 17.[433]

Azarenka, who is friends with Williams and just recently returned to the tour full-time after giving birth to a child in December 2016, has lost two U.S. Open finals to Williams in three sets. Five of those 10 Slam matches, including the last four, have needed a deciding set.[434] It will be interesting to see if the bond of motherhood deepens their friendship while they vie for titles after Williams returns.

Chapter 7: Serena Williams' Personal Life

So you have learned all about Serena Williams and the spectacular heights she has reached while climbing to the summit of her sport. While you have seen flashes of her personality and competitive fire reflected in her wins and losses, there are still many parts that comprise the whole of Serena Williams. She is more than the younger sister of Venus Williams, both on and off the court.

There is plenty of life to her, a little bit of a mischief, and as she goes forward into what may very well be the biggest year of her life without picking up a tennis racket for the rest of 2017, an entire world that will be hers for the taking.

As is the case with most professional athletes, they are thrust into the public eye as having to be "role models" for the next generation, and Williams has been no different. But in addition to being a superstar at tennis, Williams is an aspiring fashion mogul who has a signature clothing line she sells on Home Shopping Network.[435] She has her own charitable foundations, both the Serena Williams Fund and The Williams Sisters Fund, as well as the Yetunde Price Resource Center.[436]

The toughness and competitive fire were instilled at a young age as she and Venus practiced on those rundown tennis courts in Compton. Their father described it at length in sometimes shocking details in his autobiography, noting that he would bring "busloads of kids from the local schools into Compton to surround the courts while Venus and Serena practiced. I had the kids call them every curse word in the English language, including 'n-----.' I paid them to do it and told them to 'do their worst.'"[437]

There was always a free spirit to Williams as the youngest child. In that Rolling Stone piece, she admits to cheating in matches against Venus growing up and also conspired with her to cut off an older sister's braids.[438] This is still sometimes the little girl you see on the court, the one who will hop and twirl after a tournament victory and flash her megawatt smile that has so many sponsors lined up for endorsement deals.

There could have been more of that over the years had the incident at Indian Wells in 2001 not taken place. "The false allegations that our matches were fixed hurt, cut, and ripped into us deeply," she wrote in the essay for Time Magazine ahead of her 2015 return there. "The undercurrent of racism was painful, confusing, and unfair. ... I suddenly felt unwelcome, alone, and afraid."[439]

That is a lot for any professional athlete to take. Then there were all the issues with her body, especially as she battled depression following the murder of her half-sister Yetunde. There is no secret superpower she has as a tennis athlete because Williams has the same body insecurities that everyone has. In fact, some may have been exacerbated given how easy it is to ascribe different adjectives to the

6-foot-1 Venus, such as lithe and graceful, compared to Serena's 5-foot-9 frame, which is usually called "muscular" as the first or one of the first adjectives.

"I had to get comfortable with knowing that one of my weaknesses was my weight," Serena said. "Especially growing up with Venus, who's so tall and slim and model-like, and me, I'm thick hips and everything.

"I used to feel like I wanted to be her. I wanted to be thin, but it wasn't me, so I had to learn that I'm going to have larger boobs. I'm going to be bigger and just enjoy that. So I think it's good for a lot of other girls who are curvy or more bodacious to be confident in themselves."[440]

That brings us to Serena's clothing line, which is called "ANERES." She debuted back in 2003 and added a clothing collection the following year. Unlike her sister Venus, who does athletic wear, Serena opts for more casual clothing. Shortly after her debut, her company teamed up with Blue Intimates for a lingerie collection.[441]

Her deal with the Home Shopping Network gets the ANERES line seen by multiple demographics, part of an underrated business savvy Williams has displayed. Another of her successes was the ability to utilize a "see-now, buy-now" fashion show approach during the always-popular New York Fashion Week, which gave her a multimedia platform to promote her line.[442]

While dealing with racism has been a part of nearly all of Williams' life, she also has been at the forefront in combatting sexism in her sport. In March 2016, BNP Paribas tournament director Raymond Moore was rightfully blasted for his comments about women's tennis, saying that the WTA "doesn't make decisions and they are lucky," before going one enormous step further by adding that "if I was a lady player, I'd go down every night on my knees and thank God that Roger Federer and Rafa Nadal were born, because they have carried this sport. They really have."[443]

The outcry was immediate and total, and Moore eventually resigned his position in the aftermath. But it did bring up a valid point about pay discrepancy on the ATP and WTA Tours. The U.S. Open was the first to offer equal pay in prize winnings in 1973, and it took until Wimbledon did so in 2007 for all four Grand Slam events to reach that milestone.[444] Williams took the challenge for equal pay public in writing for Porter Magazine by calling out women to "break down many barriers on the road to success."

In that essay, she added the subject of equal pay "frustrates me because I know firsthand that I, like you, have done the same work and made the same sacrifices as our male counterparts I would never want my daughter to be paid less than my son for the same work. Nor would you."[445]

Her empowerment for women comes in many forms and places. She was named Sports Illustrated's Sportsperson of the Year in 2015 despite missing out on the calendar Slam, and the accompanying cover photo of her on a gold throne in a black lace bodysuit and a pair of black pumps also created a whole lot of buzz. Sports Illustrated remarked that the cover photo was "Serena's idea, to express her own ideal of femininity, strength, and power."[446]

But what made the decision of Sports Illustrated to give her the Sportsperson of the Year title was an equally provocative one that went beyond her three Grand Slam titles and near unprecedented season on the court. As editor Christian Stone put it, "we are honoring Serena Williams too for reasons that hang in the grayer, less comfortable ether, where issues such as race and femininity collide with the games."[447]

In this article, Williams recounted just how hellish 2015 was on her physically. The tendinitis in her knees, the elbow pain that hindered her serve, and the 101-degree fever that had her on the verge of withdrawing from the French Open final. But she also recalled the point where she had mentally changed. A code violation against Sharapova similar to the one she received in the 2001 U.S. Open final was met with indifference before moving on to win the next point.[448]

That maturity was also evident in the essay that marked her return to Indian Wells. She wrote three drafts, and Williams' mother Oracene Price admitted that no one wanted her to return, noting that she would not have gone back were it her. "Not because I didn't forgive them –

because of my own integrity. If they didn't think I deserve to be there? Then I don't need to be there."[449]

It was her father who first noticed her daughter's need to make that trip so many years after that tear-filled drive back to Los Angeles after winning that title. Williams' faith as a Jehovah's Witness also contributed as she leaned on the power of forgiveness.[450] This may have been the biggest factor in her parents seeing Williams as both a woman and their daughter.

"To learn to forgive: She has a problem with that," Price noted. "It's a big step for her. Because she's the kind fo person who would get revenge on you – and it was never going to end."[451]

And she used her star power for good, creating a fundraising appeal with the Equal Justice Initiative to coincide with her return. Williams raised nearly $200,000 between offering a hitting session, souvenir racket, and tickets for her first match back at Indian Wells.[452]

It was a point she now feels is her best moment in her career, strong words when you consider there are 23 Grand Slam titles and countless other trophies won in a career that is all but unprecedented in her sport.

"It released a lot of feelings that I didn't even know I had," she said. "I was really surprised at how emotional I got – and how relieved I felt after everything was said and done."[453]

Williams understands her voice stands out in this day and age and realizes she has to do more and wants to do more. But she's also aware of her place in this history, having taken on-line courses to learn about U.S. civil rights history and being disappointed in how much knowledge she lacked.[454] The hope she has that "if one person hears me, maybe that person can speak out and help. I embrace that. I'm willing and happy to be part of this new movement,"[455] is one that has slowly gained traction across both sport and celebrity.

Touching on the last part of Williams' personal life is perhaps the newest one, the whirlwind romance with Alexis Ohanian in which she will soon become his wife and mother of their first child. The two met at a chance encounter in Rome in 2014 and quietly began dating.[456]

While Williams is constantly in the public eye, Ohanian is no stranger to publicity himself. He is a titan in the internet and tech industry who came of age at just 22 when he co-founded Reddit, which has since become one of the top news aggregation websites in the world.[457] Ohanian would go on to create other social media websites and a venture capital firm before that chance meeting in Rome.

Williams recounted the day Ohanian proposed via a poem on Reddit, while Ohanian ironically took the more old-fashioned method of a simple message on his Facebook page that read "She said yes."[458]

Despite a nearly universal response of happiness from both her peers and the public regarding her pregnancy and impending nuptials, there were still some unfortunately at ease with the thought of an interracial marriage. Former tennis great Ilie Nastase made a horrific, and no pun intended here, off-color remark about Williams' pregnancy, answering a question about it with the response, "Let's see what color it has. Chocolate with milk?"[459] while in charge of the Romanian Davis Cup team.

Williams ripped into Nastase via an Instagram post, noting the larger picture of how the "world has come so far, but yet we have so much further to go."[460] Since that incident, much of Williams' social media accounts have been that of a bubbly, pregnant mother-to-be as she prepares for what will undoubtedly be another interesting chapter of her life.

Chapter 8: The Legacy of Serena Williams

Even while she trails Margaret Court by one Grand Slam title for the most of any female player in any era, it can be said that Serena Williams is the greatest female tennis player of all-time and among the greats of the sport regardless of gender.

Both she and her sister revolutionized the game with power that was unprecedented on the WTA Tour, which had only seen flashes of it in the superstars of yesteryear in Evert, Navratilova, and Graf. As much as fans hoped there would be lasting rivalries for Williams in the form of Hingis, Capriati, Henin, Clijsters, and Sharapova, it is somewhat unsurprising that in the end, the only other player who had the staying power of Serena was her sister Venus.

The 23 Grand Slam titles are a benchmark that is going to likely wind up being unassailable until well after Serena Williams' retirement. Only two other active players have at least five, Venus Williams (7) and Sharapova (5). While Sharapova has completed the career Grand Slam, Serena Williams has accomplished that feat three times over, and the only Open Era mark that is out of her reach is Evert's seven French Open titles.

Williams' pregnancy-related absence means that her legacy still has a chapter or two left to be written. While matching and potentially surpassing Court's 24 Grand Slam titles is at the top of the list, she also has the chance to set Open Era marks for most Wimbledon and U.S. Open titles. Williams needs two more at the all-England Club to match Navratilova, and her next one at Flushing Meadow will move her ahead of Evert for the most. Another win at Roland Garros would make her one of only four women with at least four French Open championships, and her seven Australian Open singles titles are three more than the closest pursuer.

But Williams' on-court legacy is not restricted to her singles play. One could write another entire section on her success with her sister in doubles. They have teamed for 14 Grand Slam titles, never losing a final in those events, which ties them for second among partners with Gigi Fernandez and Natasha Zvereva and well behind the 21 accumulated by Navratilova and Pam Shriver. The most impressive run the Williams' sisters had was from 2008-10 when they won six of a possible eight Grand Slam titles as well as the gold medal in Beijing.

If anything, the ability of the siblings' ability to play well together when trying to beat the other in singles may have contributed to their staying power. Who wants to retire when you can keep playing with your best friend?

Additionally, there may be no one better suited than Williams to add those last chapters given the impact Mouratoglou has had. Though the rumors of the two dating shortly after he became her coach have been neither confirmed nor refuted,[461] no one can deny the impact he has had in shaping the third act of her career since his arrival in 2012.

Mouratoglou is the one tennis person Williams will listen to, and if his interview with L'Equipe is any indication, he will be patient and cautious in bringing her along to be in game shape conducive enough to add to her Grand Slam totals.

"She has left the door open ... she asked me if I can wait for her. I have to reflect about it, because it's a long period, at least a year. I don't think she will be able to come back at next year's Australian Open. We can see it with Azarenka that she won't come back before Wimbledon, despite she is looking forward to. Coming back at a certain level after a such experience is not easy. She is able to do it."[462]

One part of her legacy that appears to be cemented is that she is the most celebrated female African-American athlete ever. That is partly due to the paucity of such heroes across all sports, but for tennis, African-American role models begin with U.S. Open pioneer Althea Gibson in the 1950s. While there was Arthur Ashe on the men's side to look up to, in the gap between his retirement and before Williams' arrival as a teenager, the highest-profile African-American female tennis player was Zina Garrison, who reached the 1990 Wimbledon final in singles.

There have been other sports heroes, of course. Jackie-Joyner Kersee and Florence-Griffith come immediately to mind in the 1990s, and rightfully so. But they were also out of sight and out of mind save every four years when they would represent the United States at the highest levels of their track and field events at the Olympics. And while Cheryl Miller was a standout basketball player, there was no domestic basketball league for women in America when she was at the peak of her sport.

While she has not been as outspoken as Williams, Lisa Leslie serves as a parallel trailblazer in some areas because her career coincided with the rise of the WNBA, which is now into its third decade as a professional sport. But with tennis being a year-round endeavor, Williams has never truly left the spotlight thanks to her play and words. And in today's world, there is always a news cycle eager for fresh information, or sadly sometimes, fresh controversy.

Here is where Williams has done a magnificent job rising above the fray, whether it be her championing of equal pay at more tournaments, or how she responded to Nastase's tasteless comments. Her essay returning to Indian Wells was a seminal moment for her in her life; one that went beyond tennis. Here was Williams not only recognizing that she is a role model for the young, regardless of sex or creed or orientation, but her measured words showed her as embracing the role as an African-American.

And Williams the businesswoman also helps Williams the philanthropist. What once started in Ghana has now spread to other African countries including Uganda, Kenya, and Zimbabwe.[463] The school in Kenya now enrolls more than 400 students, more than half-female as per her requirement that enrollment must be at least 40 percent female. And it has now reached an excitng inflection point in that two boys in the school have qualified for college, an unprecedented happening in the village of Wee.[464]

Her coterie has always included famous people, including Martha Stewart and Facebook executive Sheryl Sandberg, and her curiosity knows no bounds. Her ANERES clothing line, while a passion, almost acts as a conduit to her ever-expanding orbit of celebrity friends. It's not every day Vogue editor Anna Wintour takes time out of her schedule to fine-tune your clothing line, yet she did just that for Williams' first New York Fashion Week show in 2015.[465]

With her impending nuptials to Ohanian, that circle will widen further in a way that could significantly enhance Williams' charitable foundations both domestic and international. And given his tech-savvy nature, there's little doubt the message they craft will potentially be at the cutting edge of a new way to do things going forward.

There will always be the few who remember the Serena Williams moments of controversy first, whether it be the original Indian Wells saga in 2001, the iconic Puma catsuit she displayed at the 2002 U.S. Open, the Nike leopard-print suit she wore at the 2014 U.S. Open[466], or the threatening of the lineswoman at the 2009 U.S. Open. Anything and everything are fair game to be judged in a light as unique as a person's own biases who views them.

But to judge each of those things individually puts one at risk of missing the whole picture of who Serena Williams is. Regardless of status concerning fame and wealth, every human being is a complex figure full of emotions and vitality. Serena Williams is a tennis icon, a pioneer for both her sport and her race, a person who is finely attuned to history as it happens around her, and soon to be a mother and wife. She will add those unique perspectives to the already multi-colored kaleidoscope she has presented to the public in a mere 35 years.

Even if she swings a racket for only the next 3.5 years, there is an excellent chance she will be making a difference in society for a second 35 years.

Final Word/About the Author

I was born and raised in Norwalk, Connecticut. Growing up, I could often be found spending many nights watching basketball, soccer, and football matches with my father in the family living room. I love sports and everything that sports can embody. I believe that sports are one of most genuine forms of competition, heart, and determination. I write my works to learn more about influential athletes in the hopes that from my writing, you the reader can walk away inspired to put in an equal if not greater amount of hard work and perseverance to pursue your goals. If you enjoyed *Serena Williams: The Inspiring Story of One of Tennis' Greatest Legends*, please leave a review! Also, you can read more of my works on *Roger Federer, Novak Djokovic, Andrew Luck, Rob Gronkowski, Brett Favre, Calvin Johnson, Drew Brees, J.J. Watt, Colin Kaepernick, Aaron Rodgers, Peyton Manning, Tom Brady, Russell Wilson, Michael Jordan, LeBron James, Kyrie Irving, Klay Thompson, Stephen Curry, Kevin Durant, Russell Westbrook, Anthony Davis, Chris Paul, Blake Griffin, Kobe Bryant, Joakim Noah, Scottie Pippen, Carmelo Anthony, Kevin Love, Grant Hill, Tracy McGrady, Vince Carter, Patrick Ewing, Karl Malone, Tony Parker, Allen Iverson, Hakeem Olajuwon, Reggie Miller, Michael Carter-Williams, John Wall, James Harden, Tim Duncan, Steve Nash, Draymond Green, Kawhi Leonard, Dwyane Wade, Ray Allen, Pau Gasol, Dirk Nowitzki, Jimmy Butler, Paul Pierce, Manu Ginobili, Pete Maravich, Larry Bird, Kyle Lowry, Jason Kidd, David Robinson, LaMarcus Aldridge, Derrick Rose, Paul*

George, Kevin Garnett, Chris Paul, Marc Gasol, Yao Ming, Al Horford, Amar'e Stoudemire, DeMar DeRozan, Isaiah Thomas, Kemba Walker and Chris Bosh in the Kindle Store. If you love tennis, check out my website at claytongeoffreys.com to join my exclusive list where I let you know about my latest books and give you lots of goodies.

Like what you read? Please leave a review!

I write because I love sharing the stories of influential athletes like Serena Williams with fantastic readers like you. My readers inspire me to write more so please do not hesitate to let me know what you thought by leaving a review! If you love books on life, tennis, or productivity, check out my website at claytongeoffreys.com to join my exclusive list where I let you know about my latest books. Aside from being the first to hear about my latest releases, you can also download a free copy of *33 Life Lessons: Success Principles, Career Advice & Habits of Successful People*. See you there!

Clayton

References

I. Gale, Thomson. "Williams, Serena 1981-." Contemporary Black Biography. 2005. Web.

II. Williams, Serena. "My Life: Queen of the Court." 2009. Book.

III. Ibid.

IV. Ibid.

V. Ibid.

VI. Baldridge, Martin. "So You Want to Win Wimbledon?" 2014. Book.

VII. Ibid.

VIII. Gale, Thomson. "Williams, Serena 1981-." Contemporary Black Biography. 2005. Web.

IX. "Status: Undefeated. Future: Rosy. Age: 10." The New York Times. 3 July 1990. Web.

X. Ibid.

XI. Walker. "Rick Macci on his first meeting Richard, Venus and Serena Williams." 22 April 2014. Web.

XII. Macci, Rick. "Macci Magic: Extracting Greatness from Yourself and Others." 2014. Book.

XIII. Ibid.

XIV. Ibid.

XV. Baldridge, Martin. "So You Want to Win Wimbledon?" 2014. Book.

XVI. Ibid.

XVII. Ibid.

XVIII. Peebles, Maurice. "Serena Williams' Childhood Coach: She will be No. 1 in the world, or she will go to jail." Complex. 23 September 2015. Web.

XIX. Ibid.

XX. Ibid.

XXI. Gale, Thomson. "Williams, Serena 1981-." Contemporary Black Biography. 2005. Web.

XXII. Peebles, Maurice. "Serena Williams' Childhood Coach: She will be No. 1 in the world, or she will go to jail." Complex. 23 September 2015. Web.

XXIII. Finn, Robin. "A Family Tradition at 14." The New York Times. 31 October 1995. Web.

XXIV. Ibid.

XXV. Ibid.

XXVI. Ibid.

XXVII.   Ibid.
XXVIII. "Serena Williams Bio." WTA Tennis Tour, 1997. Web.
XXIX.   Ibid.
XXX.   Ibid.
XXXI.   "Serena Williams Stuns Seles." The Associated Press via The New York Times. 8 November 1997. Web.
XXXII.   Ibid.
XXXIII. Greenstein, Teddy. "Serena's Roll Stops with Davenport." Chicago Tribune. 9 November 1997.
XXXIV.   Ibid.
XXXV.   Ibid.
XXXVI.   "Serena Williams Bio." WTA Tennis Tour, 1998. Web.
XXXVII. Cart, Julie. "A Family Affair is Shaping Up in Early Rounds at Melbourne." Los Angeles Times. 20 January 1998. Web.
XXXVIII. Finn, Robin. "The Williams' Sisters First Meeting at a Grand Slam." The New York Times. 21 January, 1998. Web.
XXXIX.   Ibid.
XL.   Ibid.
XLI.   "Serena Williams Bio." WTA Tennis Tour, 1998. Web.
XLII.   Harwitt, Sandra. "Serena Williams once challenged men's player at Australian Open." USA Today. 21 January 2017. Web.
XLIII.   Ibid.
XLIV.   Ibid.
XLV.   "Serena Williams Bio." WTA Tennis Tour, 1998. Web.
XLVI.   , Rob. "Serena Williams Ousted by Sanchez Vicario." The Associated Press via Washington Post. 31 May 1998. Web.
XLVII.   Ibid.
XLVIII. Frey, Jennifer. "Injured Serena Williams Withdraws." Washington Post. 30 June 1998. Web.
XLIX.   Ibid.
L.   "Serena Williams Bio." WTA Tennis Tour, 1998. Web.
LI.   Clarey, Christopher. "One Year Later, Spirlea Defeats a Williams Sister." The New York Times. 5 September 1998. Web.
LII.   Wilstein, Steve. "Serena Overruled, Ousted." The Associated Press via Sun-Sentinel. 23 January, 1999.
LIII.   "Serena Williams Bio." WTA Tennis Tour, 1999. Web.
LIV.   Christopher, Matt. "On the Court with... Venus and Serena Williams." Google. E-Book. 2009.
LV.   "Serena Williams Bio." WTA Tennis Tour, 1999. Web.

LVI. Finn, Robin. "Moya No. 1; Serena Beats Graf in Evert." The New York Times. 14 March 1999. Web.

LVII. Finn, Robin. "Serena Williams Will Put Streak on Line Against Hingis." The New York Times. 25 March 1999. Web.

LVIII. McKee, Sandra. "Williams Sisters Serve Notice." Baltimore Sun. 27 March 1999. Web. (35)

LIX. Finn, Robin. "Williams Showdown: Venus Beats Sister Serena." The New York Times. 29 March 1999. Web.

LX. Ibid.

LXI. Dillman, Lisa. "Fernandez's Big Upset is Predictable." Los Angeles Times. 29 May 1999. Web.

LXII. "Serena Williams Bio." WTA Tennis Tour, 1999. Web.

LXIII. Ibid.

LXIV. Roberts, John. "Highs and Lows of Graf the great." The Independent. 13 August 1999. Web.

LXV. Gao, Max. "1999 U.S. Open Lookback: Serena Williams' Maiden Grand Slam Title." 28 August 2015. Web.

LXVI. "U.S. Open: Serena Williams Leaving Friendship in the Locker Room for Kim Clijsters Clash." 12 September 2009. The Telegraph. Web.

LXVII. Gao, Max. "1999 U.S. Open Lookback: Serena Williams' Maiden Grand Slam Title." 28 August 2015. Web.

LXVIII. Roberts, Selena. "Serena Williams Wins Match, Then Takes Shot at Hingis." The New York Times. 3 September 1999.

LXIX. Lupica, Mike. "On Serena's first U.S. Open title." New York Daily News. 12 September 1999. Web.

LXX. BlackNSassy pow. "Serena vs Hingis1999 US OPEN." YouTube. 26 September 2015. Web.

LXXI. BlackNSassy pow. "Serena vs Hingis1999 US OPEN pt 2." YouTube. 26 September 2015. Web.

LXXII. BlackNSassy pow. "Serena vs Hingis1999 US OPEN pt 3." YouTube. 26 September 2015. Web.

LXXIII. BlackNSassy pow. "Serena vs Hingis1999 US OPEN pt 4." YouTube. 26 September 2015. Web.

LXXIV. BlackNSassy pow. "Serena vs Hingis1999 US OPEN pt 5." YouTube. 26 September 2015. Web.

LXXV. BlackNSassy pow. "Serena vs Hingis1999 US OPEN pt 6." YouTube. 26 September 2015. Web.

LXXVI. Ibid.

LXXVII. BlackNSassy pow. "Serena vs Hingis1999 US OPEN pt 7." YouTube. 26 September 2015. Web.

LXXVIII. Ibid.

LXXIX.   BlackNSassy pow. "Serena vs Hingis1999 US OPEN pt 8."
         YouTube. 26 September 2015. Web.
LXXX.   Ibid.
LXXXI.   Ibid.
LXXXII. Finn, Robin. "Little Sister Becomes the Stardust Half." The
         New York Times. 12 September 1999. Web.
LXXXIII. Ibid.
LXXXIV. "Serena Tops Sis for Cup." Chicago Tribune. 4 October 1999.
         Web.
LXXXV.   Ibid.
LXXXVI. "Serena Williams Bio." WTA Tennis Tour, 1999. Web.
LXXXVII. "Serena Williams Bio." WTA Tennis Tour, 2000. Web. (60)
LXXXVIII. "Likhovtseva overwhelms Serena." ESPN.com. 28 January
         2000.
LXXXIX. Ibid.
XC.   "Serena Williams Bio." WTA Tennis Tour, 2000. Web.
XCI.   Ibid.
XCII.   "Serena Williams injures knee, withdraws." UPI Wire Services.
         11 April 2000. Web.
XCIII.   Wilson, Stephen. "Venus takes Wimbledon family feud." The
         Associated Press via Peninsula Clarion. 7 July 2000. Web.
XCIV.   Ibid.
XCV.   Ibid.
XCVI.   Gutierrez, Valerie. "Now It's Serena's Turn to Take Title." Los
         Angeles Times. 14 August 2000. Web.
XCVII.   Ibid.
XCVIII. Nidetz, Stephen. "Hingis wins du Maurier title as Serena retires
         with injury." Chicago Tribune. 21 August 2000. Web.
XCIX.   Roberts, Selena. "Calm Davenport Outmuscles Serena
         Willams." The New York Times. 7 September 2000. Web.
C.   Ibid.
CI.   "Williams sisters win gold in women's doubles." The
         Associated Press via ESPN.com. 28 September 2000. Web.
CII.   Ibid.
CIII.   Ibid.
CIV.   "Serena Williams Bio." WTA Tennis Tour, 2001. Web.
CV.   Parsons, John. "Australian Open: 'Chokers' Count Their
         Losses." The Telegraph. 24 January 2001. Web. (78-80)
CVI.   Ibid.
CVII.   Ibid.
CVIII.   Drucker, Joel. "What Happened at Indian Wells?" ESPN.com.
         11 March 2009. Web.

CIX.   Ibid.
CX.   Ibid.
CXI.   Dillman, Lisa. "Williams' Situation Getting Even Stickier."
          Los Angeles Times. 23 March 2001. Web. (84)
CXII.   Drucker, Joel. "What Happened at Indian Wells?" ESPN.com.
          11 March 2009. Web.
CXIII.   Ibid.
CXIV.   Ibid.
CXV.   Ibid.
CXVI.   Ibid.
CXVII.   Ibid.
CXVIII.   Ibid.
CXIX.   Ibid.
CXX.   Ibid.
CXXI.   Ibid.
CXXII.   Ibid.
CXXIII.   "Serena Williams Bio." WTA Tennis Tour, 2001. Web.
CXXIV.   Roberts, Selena. "Capriati Rally Runs Serena Off Court." The
          New York Times. 4 July 2001.
CXXV.   Ibid.
CXXVI.   "Serena Williams Bio." WTA Tennis Tour, 2001. Web.
CXXVII.   Starr, Michael. "Ladies First – Women's Final Is So Hot,
          They're Moving It to Prime Time." New York Post. 30 August
          2001. Web.
CXXVIII. Jones, Chris. "Serena Fired Up by Hingis Race Claim." The
          Evening Standard. 28 August 2001. Web.
CXXIX.   Ibid.
CXXX.   Roberts, Selena. "The Night Belongs to Venus." The New York
          Times. 9 September 2001. Web.
CXXXI.   Ibid.
CXXXII.   "Sanex Championships Transcript." ASAP Sports. 4 November
          2001.
CXXXIII. Clarey, Christopher. Agassi and Serena Williams Withdraw in
          Australia; Kuerten is Beaten." The New York Times. 14
          January 2002. Web.
CXXXIV.   Ibid.
CXXXV.   "Serena Williams Bio." WTA Tennis Tour, 2002. Web.
CXXXVI.   Parsons, John. "Serena Keeps Title in the Family." The
          Telegraph. 30 March 2002. Web.
CXXXVII. "Serena Williams Bio." WTA Tennis Tour, 2002. Web.
CXXXVIII. Ibid.

CXXXIX. "Venus, Serena sail into semis." The Associated Press via ESPN.com. 17 July 2002. Web.

CXL. "Serena Sees off Capriati." BBC Sport. 6 June 2002. Web.

CXLI. Henderson, Jon. "Sister Act Stutters Again." The Guardian. 8 June 2002. Web.

CXLII. Ibid.

CXLIII. Ibid.

CXLIV. "Serena Williams Bio." WTA Tennis Tour, 2002. Web.

CXLV. Ibid.

CXLVI. Henderson, Jon. "Sturdy Serena is sister superior." The Guardian. 7 July 2002. Web.

CXLVII. Ibid.

CXLVIII. "Serena Williams Bio." WTA Tennis Tour, 2002. Web.

CXLIX. Ibid.

CL. Garber, Greg. "Davenport: Serena's phenomenal." ESPN.com. 22 July 2002 Web.

CLI. "Serena: Three straight slams." The Associated Press via ESPN.com. 8 September 2002. Web.

CLII. Ibid.

CLIII. Ibid.

CLIV. "Serena Williams Bio." WTA Tennis Tour, 2002. Web.

CLV. "Serena scraps through to the second round." The Guardian. 14 January 2003. Web.

CLVI. Ibid.

CLVII. Clarey, Christopher. "Comeback Keeps Final in the Family." The New York Times. 24 January 2003. Web.

CLVIII. Ibid.

CLIX. Ibid.

CLX. Ibid.

CLXI. Brown, Phil. "Serena Williams beats sister, completes Serena Slam." The Associated Press via USA Today. 25 January 2003. Web.

CLXII. Ibid.

CLXIII. Ibid.

CLXIV. Ibid.

CLXV. Ibid.

CLXVI. "Serena Williams Bio." WTA Tennis Tour, 2003. Web.

CLXVII. Ibid.

CLXVIII. Pucin, Diane. "Serena's Semifinal Loss is a real crowd-pleaser." Los Angeles Times. 6 June 2003. Web.

CLXIX. Ibid.

CLXX. Ibid.

CLXXI.   "Serena Williams Bio." WTA Tennis Tour, 2003. Web.
CLXXII.   Boeck, Greg. "Serena still owns Capriati; Venus of old returns in quarters." USA Today. 2 July 2003. Web.
CLXXIII.   Mott, Sue. "Force is with Serena as she takes revenge." The Telegraph. 4 July 2003. Web.
CLXXIV.   Boeck, Greg. "Serena, injury overshadow Venus in Wimbledon final." USA Today. 5 July 2003. Web.
CLXXV.   Ibid.
CLXXVI.   Ibid.
CLXXVII.   Harris, Beth. "Serena Williams to miss U.S. Open after knee surgery." The Associated Press via USA Today. 2 August 2003. Web.
CLXXVIII. Witheridge, Anne, and Yapp, Robin. "Williams' sister dies in shooting." Daily Mail. 15 September 2003. Web.
CLXXIX.   Ibid.
CLXXX.   Hodgkinson, Mark. "Serena Williams opens up about trauma of her sister's murder." The Telegraph. 28 August 2009. Web.
CLXXXI.   Ibid.
CLXXXII.   "Serena quickly back in old routine." Reuters via CNNSport. 26 March 2004. Web.
CLXXXIII. Ibid.
CLXXXIV.   "Serena Williams Bio." WTA Tennis Tour, 2004. Web.
CLXXXV.   Bierley, Stephen. "Williams sisters are struck down in short order." The Guardian. 2 June 2004. Web.
CLXXXVI.   "Serena Williams Bio." WTA Tennis Tour 2004. Web.
CLXXXVII. Crowther, Nick. "Serena wins Mauresmo battle." BBC Sport. 1 July 2004.
CLXXXVIII. Wilson, Stephen. "Sharapova topples Williams to win Wimbledon crown." The Associated Press via USA Today. 3 July 2004. Web.
CLXXXIX.   Ibid.
CXC.   "Serena Williams Bio." WTA Tennis Tour, 2004.
CXCI.   "Serena Williams Bio." WTA Tennis Tour, 2005. Web.
CXCII.   "Williams comeback stuns Sharapova." BBC Sport. 27 January 2005. Web.
CXCIII.   Ibid.
CXCIV.   "Williams beats Davenmport." Australian Associated Press via The Age. 29 January 2005. Web.
CXCV.   Ibid.
CXCVI.   "Serena outlasts exhausted Davenport for Australian Open title." Tennis-X. 29 January 2005. Web.
CXCVII.   Ibid.

CXCVIII.	Dillman, Lisa. "Serena Pulls Out, Citing Ankle Injury." Los Angeles Times. 21 May 2005. Web. (170)
CXCIX.	Clarke, Liz. "On Grand Stage, Williamses Struggle to Return to Form." The Washington Post. 27 June 2005. Web.
CC.	Ibid.
CCI.	Ibid.
CCII.	"Serena Williams Bio." WTA Tennis Tour, 2005. Web.
CCIII.	Pagliaro, Richard. "This Date in U.S. Open History: September 4." Tennis.com. 4 September 2012. Web.
CCIV.	Ibid.
CCV.	"Sun Tiantian eclipses Serena at China Open." Agence France Presse. 22 September 2005. Web.
CCVI.	Ibid.
CCVII.	"Serena Williams Bio." WTA Tennis Tour, 2006. Web.
CCVIII.	Clarey, Christopher. "Rust and Hantuchova Catch Up to Serena Williams." The New York Times. 21 January 2006. Web.
CCIX.	Ibid.
CCX.	Ibid.
CCXI.	Williams, Serena, with Paisner, Daniel. "My Life: Queen of the Court." 2009. Pocket Books. pp 174-175. Book.
CCXII.	"Venus Williams withdraws from WTA Masters Series event." Agence France-Presse via Business Recorder. 24 March 2006. Web.
CCXIII.	"Serena Williams Bio." WTA Tennis Tour, 2006. Web.
CCXIV.	"Serena Williams returns after mental break." The Associated Press via USA Today. 13 July 2006. Web.
CCXV.	Ibid.
CCXVI.	Ibid.
CCXVII.	"Serena Williams Bio." WTA Tennis Tour, 2006.
CCXVIII.	Ibid.
CCXIX.	Fendrich, Howard. "Mauresmo beats Williams at U.S. Open." The Associated Press via Washington Post. 5 September 2006. Web.
CCXX.	"Tennis ace Serena Williams supports Ghana's biggest health campaign." UNICEF. 6 November 2006. Web.
CCXXI.	Ibid.
CCXXII.	Clarey, Christopher. "Williams is Trying to Recover the Magic." The New York Times. 14 January 2007. Web.
CCXXIII.	Ibid.
CCXXIV.	Ibid.
CCXXV.	"Serena Williams Bio." WTA Tennis Tour, 2007. Web.

CCXXVI.   "Serena makes mockery of Petrova's predicition." Sydney Morning Herald. 19 January 2007. Web.

CCXXVII.   Ibid.

CCXXVIII.   "Williams sneaks past Peer and into semifinals." Reuters via Eurosport. 23 January 2007. Web.

CCXXIX.   Ibid.

CCXXX.   Robson, Douglas. "This Serena Slam's a stunner." Los Angeles Times. 27 January 2007. Web.

CCXXXI.   Clarey, Christopher. "Williams Shocks Sharapova to win Australian Open." The New York Times. 27 January 2007. Web.

CCXXXII.   Ibid.

CCXXXIII.   Ibid.

CCXXXIV.   "Serena Williams Bio." WTA Tennis Tour, 2007. Web.

CCXXXV.   Smith, Bruce. "Groin injury forces Serena to withdraw." The Associated Press via The Washington Post. 10 April 2007. Web.

CCXXXVI.   "Serena Williams Bio." WTA Tennis Tour, 2007. Web.

CCXXXVII.   Macur, Juliet. "Serena Williams Falters and Henin Capitalizes." The New York Times. 6 June 2007. Web.

CCXXXVIII.   "Henin sends Serena crashing out." The Guardian. 4 July 2007. Web.

CCXXXIX.   Robbins. Liz." Henin Defeats Serena Again." The New York Times. 5 September 2007. Web.

CCXL.   Ibid.

CCXLI.   "Serena Williams Bio." WTA Tennis Tour, 2007. Web.

CCXLII.   Cambers, Simon. "U.S. edge out Serbia to win Hopman Cup." Reuters. 4 January 2008. Web.

CCXLIII.   Clarey, Christopher. "Serena Williams Isn't Able to Defend Her Title." The New York Times. 22 January 2008. Web.

CCXLIV.   Rajan, Sanjay. "Serena to meet Schnyder in Bangalore final." Reuters. 8 March 2008. Web.

CCXLV.   "Serena Williams Bio." WTA Tennis Tour, 2008. Web.

CCXLVI.   "Serena survivies Jankovic rally, wins fifth Sony Ericsson title." The Associated Press via ESPN.com. 6 April 2008. Web.

CCXLVII.   "Serena Williams Bio." WTA Tennis Tour, 2008. Web.

CCXLVIII.   Roopanarine, Les. "Serena suffers early exit in Paris." The Guardian. 30 May 2008. Web.

CCXLIX.   Ibid.

CCL.   Gowar, Rex. "Serena powers way into fourth final." Reuters. 3 July 2008. Web.

CCLI.   Clarey, Christopher. "All-Williams Wimbledon Final is All Venus." The New York Times. 6 July 2008. Web.
CCLII.   Ibid.
CCLIII.   Ibid.
CCLIV.   "Serena Williams Bio." WTA Tennis Tour, 2008. Web.
CCLV.   BathingwithBerko. "Serena vs. Venus in 2008 US Open Tennis – Incredible Point!" 4 September 2008. YouTube. Web. (227)
CCLVI.   Bierley, Steve. "Serena sets her sights on more titles after ninth grand slam." The Guardian. 8 September 2008. Web.
CCLVII.   "Serena Williams Bio." WTA Tennis Tour, 2008. Web.
CCLVIII. "Dementieva crushes Serena Williams at Sydney." Reuters. 15 January 2009. Web.
CCLIX.   "Williams escapes scare as Azarenka is forced to retire. The Guardian. 26 January 2009. Web.
CCLX.   "Serena rolls to 10th Grand Slam title." The Associated Press via ESPN.com. 31 January 2009. Web.
CCLXI.   Ibid.
CCLXII.   "Serena: I played because £75,000 is a lot of money to me." The Telegraph. 11 May 2009. Web.
CCLXIII. "Serena Williams beaten by Svetlana Kuznetsova." The Telegraph. 3 June 2009. Web.
CCLXIV.   Baker, Andrew. "Venus Williams blows world no. 1 Dinara Safina away." The Telegraph. 3 July 2009. Web.
CCLXV.   "Serena Williams beats Elena Dementieva in epic Wimbledon semifinal. The Guardian. 3 July 2009. Web.
CCLXVI.   Clarey, Christopher. "A Less Familiar Ending to a Final Between Sisters." The New York Times. 4 July 2009. Web.
CCLXVII. Ibid.
CCLXVIII. "Serena Williams Bio." WTA Tennis Tour, 2009. Web. (239)
CCLXIX.   "Serena Williams vs. Kim Clijsters Head to Head." SteveGTennis. Web.
CCLXX.   Robbins, Liz. "Clijsters Wins on Penalty Assessed on Williams." The New York Times. 12 September 2009. Web.
CCLXXI.   Marketersplayground. "US Open 2009 Serena disqualified against Clijsters over a Foot Fault!! HIGH QUALITY PART I." 15 September 2009. YouTube. Web.
CCLXXII. Ibid.
CCLXXIII. Ibid.
CCLXXIV. Ibid.
CCLXXV.   Robbins, Liz. "Clijsters Wins on Penalty Assessed on Williams." The New York Times. 12 September 2009. Web.

CCLXXVI.	"Serena Williams unrepentant for rant after Kim Clijsters defeat." The Telegraph. 13 September 2009. Web.
CCLXXVII.	"Serena Williams Bio." WTA Tennis Tour, 2009. Web.
CCLXXVIII.	"Serena Williams Bio." WTA Tennis Tour, 2010. Web.
CCLXXIX.	Cambers, Simon. "Serena Williams overcomes Justine Henin to win fifth Australian Open title." The Guardian. 30 January 2010. Web.
CCLXXX.	Ibid.
CCLXXXI.	"Serena Williams Bio." WTA Tennis Tour, 2010. Web.
CCLXXXII.	Garber, Greg. "Serena becomes Stosur's latest victim." ESPN.com. 2 June 2010. Web.
CCLXXXIII.	Ibid.
CCLXXXIV.	"Serena Williams Bio." WTA Tennis Tour, 2010. Web.
CCLXXXV.	Gallagher, Brendan. "Serena Williams beats Maria Sharapova to reach quarterfinals." The Telegraph. 28 June 2010. Web.
CCLXXXVI.	Coffey, Wayne. "Serena Williams routs Vera Zvonareva for fourth title at All England club." New York Daily News. 3 July 2010. Web.
CCLXXXVII.	Ibid.
CCLXXXVIII.	Mitchell, Kevin. "Serena Williams reveals details of serious foot injury." The Guardian. 2 September 2010. Web.
CCLXXXIX.	Ibid.
CCXC.	Clarey, Christopher. "Williams Was Treated for Blood Clot in Lungs." 2 March 2011. The New York Times. Web.
CCXCI.	Ibid.
CCXCII.	Briggs, Simon. "Serena Williams recovers from nightmare first set to beat Tsvetana Pironkova in comeback match at Eastbourne." The Telegraph. 3 June 2011. Web.
CCXCIII.	Ibid.
CCXCIV.	Ibid.
CCXCV.	Ibid.
CCXCVI.	"Serena Williams Bio." WTA Tennis Tour, 2011. Web.
CCXCVII.	Ibid.
CCXCVIII.	Ibid.
CCXCIX.	"Serena Williams beats Caroline Wozniacki in semi." BBC Sport. 11 September 2011. Web.
CCC.	Crouse, Karen. "Stosur Captures the Title after a Williams Outburst." The New York Times. 11 Septmber 2011. Web.
CCCI.	Ibid.
CCCII.	Ibid.
CCCIII.	Ibid.
CCCIV.	Ibid.

CCCV.	"Serena Williams Bio." WTA Tennis Tour, 2011. Web.
CCCVI.	"Injured Serena Williams pulls out of Brisbane event." CNN Sport. 5 January 2012. Web.
CCCVII.	"Five time Aussie champ Williams dumped out in straight sets by Markarova." Daily Mail. 23 January 2012. Web.
CCCVIII.	"Serena Williams Bio." WTA Tennis Tour, 2012. Web.
CCCIX.	Bishop. Greg. "Serena Williams Loses in First Round." The New York Times. 29 May 2012. Web.
CCCX.	Ibid.
CCCXI.	Ibid.
CCCXII.	Gerstner, Joanne C. "Serena Williams upset, but not crushed." EspnW. 29 May 2012. Web.
CCCXIII.	"Serena Williams Bio." WTA Tennis Tour, 2012. Web.
CCCXIV.	Henson, Mike. "Serena wins fifth singles title." BBC Sport. 7 July 2012. Web.
CCCXV.	Ibid.
CCCXVI.	"Serena Williams Bio." WTA Tennis Tour, 2012. Web.
CCCXVII.	Mairs, Gavin. "Serena Williams storms to gold medal as she thrashes Maria Sharapova in women's final." The Telegraph. 4 August 2012. Web.
CCCXVIII.	"Serena Williams Bio." WTA Tennis Tour, 2012. Web. (289)
CCCXIX.	Fagan, Kate. "Serena caps endless summer with Open title." EspnW. 10 September 2012. Web.
CCCXX.	Ibid.
CCCXXI.	"Serena Williams Bio." WTA Tennis Tour, 2013. Web.
CCCXXII.	"USA's Stephens knocks Serena out of Australian Open." The Associated Press via USA Today. 22 January 2013. Web.
CCCXXIII.	Ibid.
CCCXXIV.	Nguyen, Courtney. "Serena Williams, Victoria Azarenka face fines for Dubai withdrawals." SI.com. 21 February 2013. Web.
CCCXXV.	"Serena Williams Bio." WTA Tennis Tour, 2013. Web.
CCCXXVI.	Ibid.
CCCXXVII.	Ibid.
CCCXXVIII.	Caple, Jim. "French Open title within Serena's reach." EspnW. 6 June 2013. Web.
CCCXXIX.	Battista, Judy. "Williams Rejoices, in French, after Winning 16th Slam." The New York Times. 8 June 2013. Web.
CCCXXX.	Ibid.
CCCXXXI.	Ibid.
CCCXXXII.	Ibid.
CCCXXXIII.	"Serena Williams Bio." WTA Tennis Tour, 2013. Web.
CCCXXXIV.	Ibid.

CCCXXXV.	"Serena Williams wins windy Open." ESPN.com. 8 September 2013. Web.
CCCXXXVI.	Ibid.
CCCXXXVII.	Ibid.
CCCXXXVIII.	"Serena Williams Bio." WTA Tennis Tour, 2014. Web.
CCCXXXIX.	Bishop, Greg. "Serena Williams Diplomatic in Australian Open Defeat to Ava Ivanovic." The New York Times. 19 January 2014. Web.
CCCXL.	"Serena Williams Bio." WTA Tennis Tour, 2014. Web.
CCCXLI.	Nguyen, Courtney. "Serena Williams shocked by Garbine Muguruza in French Open second round." SI.com. 28 May 2014. Web.
CCCXLII.	Ibid.
CCCXLIII.	"Serena William crashes out at the hands of Alize Cornet in a rain-affected match." The Telegraph. 28 June 2014. Web.
CCCXLIV.	"Serena Williams Bio." WTA Tennis Tour, 2014. Web.
CCCXLV.	Ibid.
CCCXLVI.	Ackerman, McCarton. "Serena sweeps aside Wozniacki for third straight U.S. Open." USOpen.org. 7 September 2014. Web.
CCCXLVII.	Ibid.
CCCXLVIII.	"Serena retires against Cornet in Wuhan opener." The Associated Press via Tennis.com. 23 September 2014. Web.
CCCXLIX.	"Serena Williams Bio." WTA Tennis Tour, 2014. Web.
CCCL.	Casey, Phil. "Serena Williams pushed all the way by Garbine Muguruza but books her place in Australian Open quarterfinal." Press Association via Daily Mail. 26 January 2015. Web.
CCCLI.	"Serena Williams Bio." WTA Tennis Tour, 2015. Web.
CCCLII.	"Serena Williams vs. Maria Sharapova head to head." SteveGTennis. Web.
CCCLIII.	McCarvel, Nick. "Serena Williams beats Maria Sharapova for Australian Open title." USA Today. 31 January 2015. Web.
CCCLIV.	Ibid.
CCCLV.	Ibid.
CCCLVI.	Williams, Serena. "I'm going back to Indian Wells." Time Magazine. 4 February 2015. Web.
CCCLVII.	Ibid.
CCCLVIII.	"Shamil Tarpischev forced to apologize for calling Williams sisters 'brothers.'" Press Association via The Guardian. 21 October 2014. Web.

CCCLIX.   Williams, Serena. "I'm going back to Indian Wells." Time
          Magazine. 4 February 2015. Web.
CCCLX.   "Simona Halep became the first player into the final of the
          BNP Paribas Open, advancing when Serena Williams had to
          withdraw from their semifinal with a right knee injury." WTA
          Tour. 20 March 2015. Web.
CCCLXI.   "Serena Williams Bio." WTA Tennis Tour, 2015. Web.
CCCLXII. Ibid.
CCCLXIII. Cambers, Simon. "Serena Williams beats Sloane Stephens to
          reach French Open last eight." The Guardian. 1 June 2015.
          Web.
CCCLXIV. "Serena Williams beats Lucie Safarova for 20th major singles
          trophy." The Associated Press via Syracuse.com. 6 June 2015.
          Web.
CCCLXV.   Ibid.
CCCLXVI. "Serena Williams Bio." WTA Tennis Tour, 2015. Web.
CCCLXVII. Newbery, Piers. "Serena Williams beats Venus to reach last
          eight." BBC Sport. 6 July 2015. Web.
CCCLXVIII. Ibid.
CCCLXIX. Ibid.
CCCLXX.   "Serena Williams Bio." WTA Tennis Tour, 2015. Web.
CCCLXXI. Clarey, Christopher. "Serena Williams Defeats Garbiñe
          Muguruza and Closes In on Grand Slam." The New York
          Times. 11 July 2015. Web.
CCCLXXII. Ibid.
CCCLXXIII. Ibid.
CCCLXXIV. "Serena Williams Bio." WTA Tennis Tour, 2015. Web.
CCCLXXV. Rothenberg, Ben. "US Open Draw Unveils Serena Williams's
          Grand Slam Path." The New York Times. 27 August 2015.
          Web.
CCCLXXVI. Rothenberg, Ben. "Injured Vitalia Diatchenko Shows
          Retirement Has Its Perks." The New York Times. 1 September
          2015. Web.
CCCLXXVII. Ibid.
CCCLXXVIII. Kalland, Robby. "Serena Williams drops first set, rallies to win
          match." CBS Sports. 4 September 2015. Web.
CCCLXXIX. Lutz, Tom. "Serena Williams strolls past Madison Keys: As it
          happened." The Guardian. 6 September 2015. Web.
CCCLXXX. Allnutt, Tom. "Serena Williams sets up quarter-final with sister
          Venus as calender slam remains on." The Independent. 7
          September 2015. Web.
CCCLXXXI. Ibid.

CCCLXXXII. Lawrence, Jesse. "Ticket Prices Jump for Serena and Venus Williams' U.S. Open Matchup." Forbes. 8 September 2015. Web.

CCCLXXXIII. Graham, Bryan Armen. "Serena Williams edges Venus in three – as it happened." The Guardian. 8 September 2015. Web.

CCCLXXXIV. Ibid.

CCCLXXXV. Ibid.

CCCLXXXVI. Ibid.

CCCLXXXVII. McCarvel, Nick. "Serena Williams beats Venus Williams to reach U.S. Open semifinals." USA Today. 8 September 2015. Web.

CCCLXXXVIII. "Serena Williams vs. Roberta Vinci head to head." SteveGTennis. Web.

CCCLXXXIX. Rothenberg, Ben. "Eugenie Bouchard Forced to Withdraw from U.S. Open." The New York Times. 6 September 2015. Web.

CCCXC. Bondy, Stefan. "Serena Williams, upset in U.S. Open by unseeded Roberta Vinci, ending quest for historic calendar Grand Slam." New York Daily News. 12 September 2015. Web.

CCCXCI. Ostlere, Lawrence. "Serena Williams beaten by Roberta Vinci – as it happened." The Guardian. 11 September 2015. Web.

CCCXCII. Ibid.

CCCXCIII. Ibid.

CCCXCIV. Clarey, Christopher. "Roberta Vinci Ends Serena Williams' Grand Slam Bid at U.S. Open." The New York Times. 11 September 2015. Web.

CCCXCV. Ibid.

CCCXCVI. Clarey, Christopher. "Serena Williams's Conspicuous Absence Strikes the WTA Finals." The New York Times. 24 October 2015. Web.

CCCXCVII. Ibid.

CCCXCVIII. Wertheim, Jon. "Angelique Kerber stuns Serena Williams to win 2016 Australian Open." SI.com. 30 January 2016. Web.

CCCXCIX. "Serena Williams Bio." WTA Tennis Tour, 2016. Web.

CD. Culpepper, Chuck. "Garbiñe Muguruza powers past Serena Williams in French Open final." The Washington Post. 4 June 2016. Web.

CDI. Ibid.

CDII. "Serena Williams Bio." WTA Tennis Tour, 2016. Web.

CDIII. Pearce, Linda. "Serena beats Angelique Kerber to claim 22nd major title." Sydney Morning Herald. 10 July 2016. Web.

CDIV.   Ibid.
CDV.   "Serena Williams Bio." WTA Tennis Tour, 2016. Web.
CDVI.   Graham, Bryan Armen. "Serena Williams out of US Open with shock loss to Karolina Pliskova." The Guardian. 8 September 2016. Web.
CDVII.   Briggs, Simon. "Serena and Venus win Australian Open semis to set up first Williams-sisters grand slam final in eight years." The Telegraph. 26 January 2017. Web.
CDVIII.   Ibid.
CDIX.   Ibid.
CDX.   Clarey, Christopher. "Serena Williams Beats Venus Williams to Win Her 7th Australian Open Title." The New York Times. 28 January 2017. Web.
CDXI.   Ibid.
CDXII.   Graham, Bryan Armen. "Serena Williams Beats Venus Williams to win the Australian Open – as it happened." The Guardian. 28 January 2017. Web.
CDXIII.   Ibid.
CDXIV.   Clarey, Christopher. "Serena Williams Beats Venus Williams to Win Her 7th Australian Open Title." The New York Times. 28 January 2017. Web.
CDXV.   Rafferty. Scott. "Serena Williams Reveals She Accidentally Announced Her Pregnancy." Rolling Stone. 26 April 2017. Web.
CDXVI.   Ibid.
CDXVII.   Clarey, Christopher. "Serena Williams's Coach Sees a 'Fabulous' New Challenge in Her Pregnancy." The New York Times. 21 April 2017. Web.
CDXVIII.   Ibid.
CDXIX.   Hardingham-Gill, Tamara. "Pregnant Serena Williams looks radiant as she poses in a dress from her signature collection." Mirror. 9 June 2017. Web.
CDXX.   "Serena Williams vs. Venus Williams Head to Head." SteveGTennis. Web.
CDXXI.   Ibid.
CDXXII.   "Serena Williams vs. Martina Hingis Head to Head." SteveGTennis. Web.
CDXXIII.   Finn, Robin. "Capriati Is Arrested in Drug Charge." The New York Times. 17 May 1994. Web.
CDXXIV.   "Serena Williams vs. Jennifer Capriati Head to Head." SteveGTennis. Web.
CDXXV.   Ibid.

CDXXVI.   Broussard, Chris. "Williams Receives Apology and Umpire's Open Is Over." The New York Times. 9 September 2004. Web.

CDXXVII.   "Serena Williams vs. Justine Henin Head to Head." SteveGTennis. Web.

CDXXVIII. Tandon, Kamakshi. "The Woman Who Had the Nerve to Beat Serena at 3 Straight Majors." EspnW. 5 September 2015. Web.

CDXXIX.   "Serena Williams vs. Maria Sharapova Head to Head." SteveGTennis. Web.

CDXXX.   Rodrick, Stephen. "Serena Williams: The Great One." Rolling Stone. 18 June 2013. Web.

CDXXXI.   "Maria Sharapova Blasts Serena Williams, Criticizes Her Love Life." Agence France Presse via Business insider. 22 June 2013. Web.

CDXXXII.   "Serena says she apologized to Sharapova over comments." The Associated Press via USA Today. 23 June 2013. Web.

CDXXXIII. "Serena Williams vs. Victoria Azarenka Head to Head." SteveGTennis. Web.

CDXXXIV.   Ibid.

CDXXXV.   Snyder, Benjamin. "After U.S. Open loss, Serena Williams turns to fashion at NYFW." Fortune. 16 September 2015. Web.

CDXXXVI.   "Serena Williams." SerenaWilliams.com. Web.

CDXXXVII. Rankine, Claudia. "The Meaning of Serena Williams." The New York Times Magazine." 25 August 2015. Web.

CDXXXVIII. Rodrick, Stephen. "Serena Williams: The Great One." Rolling Stone. 18 June 2013. Web.

CDXXXIX.   Williams, Serena. "I'm going back to Indian Wells." Time Magazine. 4 February 2015. Web.

CDXL.   Rodrick, Stephen. "Serena Williams: The Great One." Rolling Stone. 18 June 2013. Web.

CDXLI.   Willias, Alexandra. "Five Things about Serena Williams's clothing line ANERES." 16 August 2012. The Tennis Space. Web.

CDXLII.   Novellino, Teresa. "Serena Williams hits sweet spot with see-now, buy-now at Fashion Week." 12 September 2016. Web.

CDXLIII.   Ubah, Ravi and Grez, Matias. "WTA: 'Alarming' comments by Indian Wells tournament director under review." CNN Sport. 21 March 2016. Web.

CDXLIV.   Rothenberg, Ben. "Roger Federer, $731,000; Serena Williams, $495,000: The Pay Gap in Tennis." The New York Times. 12 April 2016. Web.

CDXLV. Williams, Serena. "'We must continue to dream big': an open letter from Serena Williams. The Guardian. 29 November 2016. Web. (416)

CDXLVI. Renee, Shana. "The Power of Serena Williams' Sports Illustrated cover." EspnW. 16 December 2015. Web.

CDXLVII. Stone, Christian. "Why Serena Williams is SI's 2015 Sportsperson of the Year." SI.com. 14 December 2015. Web.

CDXLVIII. Price, S.L. "Serena Williams is Sports Illustrated's 2015 Sportsperson of the Year." SI.com. 14 December 2015. Web.

CDXLIX. Ibid.

CDL. Ibid.

CDLI. Ibid.

CDLII. Ibid.

CDLIII. Ibid.

CDLIV. Ibid.

CDLV. Ibid.

CDLVI. Michael, Tom, and Chrismas, Warren. "Who is Alexis Ohanian? Reddit co-founder expecting a baby with tennis champ fiancée Serena Williams." The Sun. 4 June 2017. Web.

CDLVII. Ibid.

CDLVIII. Ibid.

CDLIX. "Ilie Nastase apologizes and says Serena Williams comment was 'spontaneous.'" The Guardian. 28 April 2017. Web.

CDLX. Williams, Serena. "serenawilliams." Instagram. 24 April 2017. Web.

CDLXI. Briggs, Simon. "Serena Williams: I don't want my engagement to cause me to lose my edge." The Telegraph. 14 January 2017. Web.

CDLXII. Luigi, Gatto. "Patrick Mouratoglou about Serena Williams: I didn't know until about 15 days ago." L'Euipe via Tennis World USA. 23 April 2017. Web.

CDLXIII. Price, S.L. "Serena Williams is Sports Illustrated's 2015 Sportsperson of the Year." SI.com. 14 December 2015. Web.

CDLXIV. Ibid.

CDLXV. Bourne, Leah. "Anna Wintour is Serena Williams' Fairy Fashion Godmother." New York Post. 15 September 2015. Web.

CDLXVI. Arth, Susie. "Some Slammin' Serena Williams Fashion: Then and Now." EspnW. 10 July 2015. Web.

Made in the USA
Las Vegas, NV
08 December 2022

61350675R00098